An Exaltation of Skylarks

photograph by Roger Wilmshurst

An Exaltation of Skylarks

in prose and poetry

devised and compiled by

Stewart Beer

SMH BOOKS

British Library Cataloguing in Publication Data

A catalogue record for this book is available from the
British Library.

ISBN 0 9512619 7 5

First published 1995 by
SMH BOOKS
Pear Tree Cottage, Watersfield, Pulborough,
West Sussex, RH20 1NG

Typeset by
St. Leonard's Press, Exeter

Printed and bound in Great Britain by
Hillman Printers (Frome) Ltd

CONTENTS

ACKNOWLEDGEMENTS

We acknowledge, with thanks, the granting of permissions for copyright passages to be reproduced here, by the following publishers, agents and persons:

The Four Courts Press, Dublin (for an anonymous poem of the 8th-10th Century, translated by Robin Flower, in A TREASURY OF IRISH RELIGIOUS VERSE); International Thompson Publishing Services Ltd. (for two extracts from A CELTIC MISCELLANY, translated by Kenneth Hurlstone Jackson, Routledge & Kegan Paul, 1951); Penguin Books Ltd. (for 'Daybreak' by Uejima Onitsura, from THE PENGUIN BOOK OF JAPANESE VERSE, 1964, translated by Geoffrey Bownas and Anthony Thwaite); Palladour Books, Aberporth, for 'Shelley in the Trenches' by Sgt. John William Streets, and 'Last Song' by 2nd Lt. Henry Lamont Simpson, reproduced from A DEEP CRY, A Literary Pilgrimage to the Battlefields and Cemeteries of First World War British Soldier-Poets Killed in Northern France and Flanders, edited and introduced by Anne Powell, 1993); Random House UK Ltd. (for extracts from NATURE'S CHANGING COURSE by E.L. Grant Watson, Hutchinson, 1961, and from WATCHER IN THE WILD by W.R. Calvert, Hutchinson, 1945); Harper Collins (for an extract from 'Lark Ascending' by Edmund Blunden, from POEMS OF MANY YEARS, Collins, 1957); Sinclair Stevenson (for 'The Ecstatic' by Cecil Day Lewis, from THE COLLECTED POEMS OF C. DAY LEWIS, Jonathan Cape. 1954); David Higham Associates (for extracts from two books by B.B. [D.J. Watkins-Pitchford]: THE QUIET FIELDS, Michael Joseph, 1981, and INDIAN SUMMER, Michael Joseph, 1984); A. & C. Black (for the Author's Preface by Diana Spearman to THE ANIMAL ANTHOLOGY, John Baker, 1966);

Arthur H. Stockwell Ltd. (for extracts from A BELL IN ITS THROAT by Gail Carter Lott, 1979, and from THE SKYLARK AND THE STEEPLEJACK by James Herne, 1933); John Murray (for 'Splendour on the Links' by John Betjeman, from his Collected Poems, A FEW LATE CHRYSANTHEMUMS, 1954); Oxford University Press (for 'Allotments', from Bernard Spencer's COLLECTED POEMS, edited by Roger Bowen, © Mrs. Anne Humphries, 1981); Punch 150 (for 'The Birds' by Clive Sansom, featured in a 1948 issue of *Punch* Magazine); Macmillan Publishing Company, New York (for an extract from EYES AND NO EYES by Arabella B. Buckley, Cassell & Co., 1911); David Higham Associates for 'Poem in October' by Dylan Marais Thomas, from DYLAN THOMAS: COLLECTED POEMS 1934-1953, edited by Professors Walford Davies and Ralph Maud, (J.M. Dent & Sons Ltd., 1988); Reed Consumer Books (for 'Song' by Ronald Duncan, from his COLLECTED POEMS, Heinemann/Quixote Press, 1981); Faber and Faber Limited (for 'Adam and the Sacred Nine: The Skylark Came' by Ted Hughes, from MOORTOWN, 1979); Random House UK Limited (for 'Praying' by P.J. Kavanagh, from SELECTED POEMS, (Chatto & Windus, 1982); Elizabeth Taggart, at J.G. Ferguson Publishing, Chicago, (for 'Larks' by Matthew J. Brennan) Volume 3, ILLUSTRATED LIBRARY OF NATURE, H.S. Stuttman, USA, 1971); Curtis Brown (for 'Skylark', from BASIL EDE'S BIRDS, text by Robert Dougal, Severn House, 1980, © Robert Dougal); *The Field* (for 'Larks and ladys' hawk', featured in 'Country Sportsman's Diary', in a 1982 issue), and Marshall Cavendish Picture Library (for 'The Skylark', from the partwork *Country Companion*, 1989).

Many copyright-holders have generously given us permission to reproduce material free of charge. In this respect, we are especially grateful to Mrs. Myfanwy Thomas (for her father's [Edward Thomas'] poem 'Good-Night', from SELECTED POEMS, Selwyn

& Blount, 1920, and Faber and Faber Ltd., 1936 and 1969); Mr. George Sassoon (for his father's [Siegfried Sassoon's] 'Suicide in the Trenches', Wayland Publishing, 1988); Mrs. Jane Youngs (for her father's [Frank Prewett's] 'The Somme Valley, 1917', from GEORGIAN POETRY, 1922, The Poetry Bookshop, 1922); Lady Marilyn Quennell (for her husband's [Peter Courtney Quennell's] 'Perception', also from GEORGIAN POETRY, 1920-22, as above); Mr. Ralph Whitlock (for 'The Sky-lark', from WILD LIFE ON THE FARM, The Falcon Press, 1953); Mr. Bob Holmes (for 'A Skylark and a Merlin, from MY COUNTRY YEAR, Quest [Western] Publications, N. Devon, 1987) and Mr. H.C.E. Noyes (for his father's [Alfred Noyes'] 'The Skylark Caged', from his COLLECTED POEMS (Wm. Blackwood & Sons Ltd., 1929).

For helping us both promptly and substantially, we especially thank Hazel Bannister, of The Society of Authors, and Dr. David Sutton, of W.A.T.C.H. (Writers and their Copyright Holders), based at the library of the University of Reading.

14

PREFACE

Out of the great and eloquent chorus of songbirds, two species above all others have captured poets' imaginations for more than two thousand years, at least: the nightingale and the skylark.

It is an odd pairing, when you think about it – one, a bird of dark and woodland, the other, of sun and air. Yet maybe it is their shared aura of otherness, the near-invisibility given by darkness and the immense spaciousness of the sky, that has enabled us to project on to them our own yearnings for freedom. As Wordsworth says in *The Plea* (quoted here), 'A wilderness is rich with liberty'. A bird which sings as it mounts up towards the sun could not fail to inspire the most exultant dreams of all – of flight, escape, transcendence.

Yet these exuberant skirlings – which, literally, are incomprehensible to us – can unlock all kinds of responses, as Stewart Beer's remarkable anthology shows. The anonymous Celt who applauded, directly and passionately, that 'timid persistent frail creature [singing] at the top of his voice', is instantly sympathetic a millennium later. The Sixteenth and Seventeenth Century poets, seeing the song as a symbol of the Ascension, or a kind of matins, are more remote but still charming.

By the Eighteenth Century, writers were listening and looking more directly, both at the bird and at their own feelings. Shelley's *Hail to thee, blythe spirit* is the most famous salute; Meredith's *The Lark Ascending* ('it drops the silver chains of sound'), a sort of skylark's song itself.

15

However, it is an extraordinary, modernist, unsigned poem from two centuries before ('The Lark', page 41) that most perfectly catches bird and song:

Throned on the welkin's crest, her voice the stair
Stills with her wings, and here becomes a chair
Where seated, in a calm, sweet strain she sings.
A loss to earth, without her tongue or wings.

John Clare (and Enid Blyton, surprisingly) saw the paradox of the drab brown ploughman's birds behind the rapture. Christina Rossetti meditated on the patience of the waiting mate in the furrows. The First World War poets heard England and survival: larks are there, alongside the Flanders fields poppies, in the bitter verse of John McCrae that inspired Remembrance Sunday. And thirty years before, anticipating Rupert Brooke, Thomas Hardy wrote about a particular lark, the lark that Shelley heard, now 'A pinch of unseen, unguarded dust…Maybe it rests in the loam I view'.

The *real* birds matter. Skylarks are not just symbols. 'An exaltation' is not just a happy epithet for their song, and for Stewart Beer's celebration of it, but is the collective word for a gathering of larks – now a scarcer and scarcer thing. In 1993, a quarter of a million occupied nests of this one-time farmer's friend were ploughed into oblivion, because of the agricultural policies whose links with the seasonal rhythms of the land are shattered.

We should listen to skylarks' songs with a new humility now. Slowed down sixteen times, there is a strange, beautifully alien music in them – 200 notes per second; exquisite arpeggios; not at all the familiar, distant trilling over the downs but a song structured as complexly, the composer David Hindley believes, as a work by Haydn or Mozart. We must respect the birds' independence, and be

16

thankful that missing from this inspiring collection (and it is all that is missing) are the unwritten, unwritable poems that skylarks sing to each other.

18

INTRODUCTION

Between the covers of this book lies evidence enough that the skylark has long drawn, and continues to draw a veritable flood of adulation. Yet, when I first planned the anthology, I started with just a handful of references. Did I, then, really expect to find enough material for a full-length work? Written celebration, I felt sure, must abound and in the course of time, a careful and constant search would garner sufficient material. So it proved.

Addictive research followed, and my confidence was rewarded. I gathered in batches of poetry and prose from the rich seams of our literary heritage.

The wealth of good material discovered, spanning many centuries, has deepened my knowledge of authors, poets and writers on nature. We are all greatly indebted to them for such varied, often erudite interpretations of their pleasure on hearing the skylark. We must also be repulsed by Robert Leighton's *The Bunch of Larks* (see page XXX). Man can turn blessedness into sordidness - one mouthful out of such a thing of beauty! Certainly for palates such as Samuel Pepys', 'a dish of larks was second only to a venison pasty...'.

From Theocritus, writing in the Third Century B.C., and translations from the early Celtic Literatures, I have drawn up a 'roll call' of illustrious writers - Chaucer and Shakespeare to George Meredith and Cecil Day-Lewis, taking in poets such as Thomas Gray, Wordsworth, Coleridge, Emily Brontë, Shelley and Blake along the way. John Clare, the Northamptonshire nature poet, is well-represented, as is Gerald Manley Hopkins, the Nineteenth-Century priest-poet, whose originality continues to shine like a beacon.

The great Skylark poems by Shelley and Wordsworth have, almost from the time of their conception, vied for literary supremacy (although I think George Meredith's *The Lark Ascending* closely challenges these works in importance).

My selection - very much a personal one - includes pieces by many lesser-known bird-lovers. W. Warde Fowler, Westell, Watson, and others, write with authority, and in refreshing ways. As Viscount Grey of Fallodon notes in the Preface to his perennial work *The Charm of Birds* (see page 131):

> After all, it is not entirely to exchange information that lovers of birds converse together on this subject. An artist will paint the commonest object in order to bring out some aspect that has particularly struck him. So with watchers of birds, some are attracted by one aspect of a well-known species and some, by another. Thus, even those of us who have nothing new to tell, may have something that is fresh to say.

Richard Jefferies reached new heights of keen observation in his nature-writing. He greatly influenced Henry Williamson (author of the classic *Tarka the Otter*). Williamson saw active service in the 'War to end all Wars' [World War I] with a number of soldier-poets and fellow-writers who, on describing the heartening songs of skylarks over the trenches and shell-pocked battlefields, have left for all time poignant, tear-spattered images of that living hell. In peace, as in war, the skylark's exuberant outpouring of joyous song enlivens the spirit. People from all walks of life are able to describe, in vivid detail, some past event when our minstrel made an indelible impression.

A close friend, now in his ninety-third year, can recall, some seventy-six years later, every detail of the time and place of his first encounter with a skylark. At the very mention of 'skylark', the bird's joyous song, while mounting the air over the golf links, echoes again in his ears. He has had many friends (Cecil Day-Lewis was one of them) with similar experiences of how'…the lark could scarce get out his notes for joy' (Tennyson).

Lifelong passions for natural history, the countryside and related literature have all been fused in my tribute to this inimitable bird. *Hail to thee, blithe spirit!*

S.B.
Pilton, Devon
March, 1995

The Harvest Festival

...On the shady boughs the dusky cicadas were busy with their chatter, and the tree-frog far off cried in the dense thorn-brake. Larks and finches sang, the dove made moan, and bees flitted humming above the springs. All things were fragrant of rich harvest and fruit time...

Theocritus (c. 310–250 B.C.)

The lark

Learned in music sings the lark,
I leave my cell to listen;
His open beak spills music, hark!
Where Heaven's bright cloudlets glisten.

And so I'll sing my morning psalm
That God bright Heaven may give me
And keep me in eternal calm
And from all sin relieve me.

Anon. (8th–10th Century)
transl. Robin Flower (1881–1946)

May-time

May-time, fair season, perfect is its aspect then; blackbirds sing a full song, if there be a scanty beam of day.

The hardy, busy cuckoo calls, welcome noble summer! It calms the bitterness of bad weather, the branching wood is a prickly hedge.

Summer brings low the little stream, the swift herd makes for the water, the long hair of the heather spreads out, the weak white cotton-grass flourishes.

...The smooth sea flows, season when the ocean falls asleep; flowers cover the world.

Bees, whose strength is small, carry with their feet a load reaped from the flowers; the mountain allures the cattle, the ant makes a rich meal.

The harp of the wood plays melody, its music brings perfect peace; colour has settled on every hill, haze on the lake of full water.

The corncrake clacks, a strenuous bard; the high pure waterfall sings a greeting to the warm pool; rustling of rushes has come.

Light swallows dart on high, brisk music encircles the hill, tender rich fruits bud...

...The hardy cuckoo sings, the speckled fish leaps, mighty is the swift warrior.

The vigour of men flourishes, the glory of great hills is unspoiled; every wood is fair from crest to ground, fair each great goodly field.

Delightful is the season's splendour, winter's rough wind has gone; bright is every fertile wood, a joyful peace is summer.

A flock of birds settles...; the green field re-echoes, where there is a brisk bright stream.

A mad ardour upon you to race horses, where the serried host is ranged around; very splendid is the bounty of the cattle-pond, the iris is gold because of it.

A timid persistent frail creature sings at the top of his voice, the lark chants a clear tale - excellent May-time of calm aspect.

Irish; author unknown
(9th–10th Century)

from **Piers the Plowman**

The lark that is a little fowl is lovelier of voice
And faster by far of wing, swifter than the peacock,
And of flesh by many-fold fatter and sweeter,
To men of lowly life, the lark is compared.
Aristotle, the great author, has told such tales,
For in his *Logic*, he used even the least of birds.

William Langland
(c. 1332–c. 1400)

from **The knight's tale**

(i)

The bisy larke, messager of day,
Salueth in hir song the morwe gray...

The Sonday night, er day bigan to springe,
Whan Palamon the larke herde singe,
(Although it nere nay day by houres two,
Yet song the larke) and Palamon right tho
With hooly herte and with an heigh corage,
He roos to wenden on his pilgrimage
Unto the blisful Citherea benigne –
I mene Venus, honurable and digne.

from **Troilus and Criseyde**

What mighte or may the sely larke seye,
Whan that the sparhauk hath it in his foot?
I can no more, but of this ilke tweye,
To whom this tale sucre be or soot.
Though that I tane a year, som tyme I mort,
After myn actor, tellen her gladnesse,
As well as I have told her hevinesse.

Geoffrey Chaucer
(c. 1340?–1400)

from **Devotion of the fowls**

The lark also full naturally,
Christ's ascension in humanity
Commended with song specially,
And said, 'Blessed be thou, Lord of felicity,
Thou hast called man to so high degree,

That never deserved of equity,
Eterne rex altissime.'

John Lydgate
(c.1370–c.1450)

Mirth of May

Richt as the stern of day began to shine,
When gone to bed was Vesper and Lucine,
  I rose, and by a rosere did me rest;
Up sprang the goldin candil matutine,
With clear depurit beamis crystallin
  Glading the mirry fowlis in their nest;
  Or Phœbus was in purpour cape revest,
Up rose the lark, the heavenis minstrel fine,
  In May, in till a morrow mirthfullest.

Full angelic the birdis sang their hours,
Within their courtings' green, within their bowers,
  Apparellit with white and red, with bloomis sweet;
Enamelit was the field with all colours,
The pearly dropis shook in silver showers,
  While all in balm did branch & leavis fleit,
  Depart fra Phoebus, did Aurora greet;
Her crystall tears I saw hung on the flowers,
  While he for love all drank up with his heat.

For mirth of May, with skipis & with hops
The birdis sang upon the tender crops
  With curious notes, as Venus chapel-clerks.
The roses red, now spreading of their knops,

Were powdered bricht with heavenly beryal drops,
Through beamis red, leming as ruby sparks;
The skyes rang for shouting of the larks,
The purpour heaven, ourscalit in silver slops,
Ourgilt the trees, branchis, leavis, and barks.

William Dunbar
(1460–c.1520)

Song of the rose

Then all the birdis sang with voice on height,
  Whose mirthful sound was marvellous to hear;
The mavis sang, "Hail, ROSE, most rich and right,
  That does up flourish under Phoebus' sphere;
  Hail, plant of youth; hail, Princess, daughter dear;
Hail, blossom breaking out of the blood royal,
  Whose precious virtue is imperial."

The merle she sang, "Hail, ROSE of most delight,
  Hail, of all flowers queen and sovereign:"
The lark she sang, "Hail, ROSE, both red and white,
  Most pleasant flower, of mighty colours twane:"
  The nightingale sang, "Hail, Nature's suffrage,

In beauty, nurture, and every nobles,
In rich array, renown, and gentleness."

William Dunbar

The mansion of the woods
'A Welsh ballad to the air: *Aboute the Banck of Elicon*'

They have sent forth their cry, the loquacious lads, yesterday they heard it under the green trees, pure and church-like, three lifetimes to the gentle laureate poets - the linnet from the brake, the blameless nightingale, solemn and celestial; the pure-toned thrush, sweet rascal; the blackbird, he whose zeal is greater; and the woodlark soaring wantonly, catching the skylark's tune; singing, scattering so much fancy, so gay, so fresh, the accent of true passion.

Anon.

The lively lark stretched forth her wing

The lively lark stretched forth her wing,
The messenger of morning bright,
And with her cheerful voice did sing
The day's approach, discharging night,
  When that Aurora, blushing red,
  Descried the guilt of Thetis' bed.

I went abroad to take the air,
And in the meads I met a knight,
Clad in carnation colour fair.
I did salute this gentle wight;
  Of him I did his name enquire.
  He sighed, and said 'I am Desire'.

Desire I did desire to stay;
Awhile with him I craved to talk.
The courteous knight said me no nay,
But hand in hand with me did walk.
  Then of Desire I asked again
  What thing did please, and what did pain.

He smiled, and thus he answered then:
'Desire can have no greater pain
Than for to see another man
That he desireth, to obtain;
  Nor greater joy can be than this,
  Than to enjoy that others miss'.

Edward de Vere, Earl Of Oxford
(1550–1604)

from **Epithalamion**

Hark how the cheerfull birds do chaunt their lays
And carol of love's praise.
The merry lark her matins sings aloft,
The thrush replies, the mavis descant plays,
The ousel shrills, the ruddock warbles soft,
So goodly all agree with sweet consent,
To this day's merriment.
Ah, my dear love, why do ye sleep thus long,
When meeter were that ye should now awake,
T'await the coming of your joyous make,
And hearken to the birds' love-learnèd song,
The dewy leaves among?
For they of joy and pleasance to you sing,
That all the woods them answer and their echo ring.

Edmund Spenser
(1552–1598)

Song from 'Cymbeline'

Hark! hark! the lark at heaven's gate sings,
  And Phoebus 'gins arise,
His steeds to water at those springs
On chaliced flowers that lies;
And winking Mary-buds begin
To ope their golden eyes;
With every thing that pretty bin:
My lady sweet, arise;
Arise, arise.

William Shakespeare
(1564–1616)

31

Lark on high

Lo! here the gentle lark, weary of rest,
From his moist cabinet mounts up on high,
And wakes the morning, from whose silver breast
The sun ariseth in his majesty;
  Who doth the world so gloriously behold
  The cedar-tops and hills seem burnish'd gold.

William Shakespeare

Spring and winter

When daisies pied, and violets blue,
    And lady-smocks all silver-white
And cuckoo-buds of yellow hue
    Do paint the meadows with delight,
The cuckoo then, on every tree,
Mocks married men, for thus sings he,
        Cuckoo;
Cuckoo, cuckoo, – O word of fear,
Unpleasing to a married ear!

When shepherds pipe on oaten straws,
    And merry larks are ploughmen's clocks,
When turtles tread, and rooks, and daws,
    And maidens bleach their summer smocks,
The cuckoo then, on every tree,
Mocks married men, for thus sings he,
        Cuckoo;
Cuckoo, cuckoo, – O word of fear,
Unpleasing to a married ear!

32

When icicles hang by the wall,
    And Dick the shepherd blows his nail,
And Tom bears logs into the hall,
    And milk comes frozen home in pail,
When blood is nipped, and ways be foul,
Then nightly sings the staring owl,
        To-whit;
    To-who, a merry note,
While greasy Joan doth keel the pot.

When all around the wind doth blow,
    And coughing drowns the parson's saw,
And birds sit brooding in the snow,
    And Marian's nose looks red and raw,
When roasted crabs hiss in the bowl,
Then nightly sings the staring owl,
        To-whit,
    To-who, a merry note,
While greasy Joan doth keel the pot.

William Shakespeare

Nature's accord

How is't each bough a several music yields?
The lusty throstle, early nightingale,
Accord in tune, though vary in their tale;
The chirping swallow call'd forth by the sun,
And crested lark doth his divisions run?
The yellow bees the air with murmur fill,
The finches carol, and the turtles bill?
Whose power is this? what god?

Ben Johnson
(1574–1637)

Daybreak

See, the day begins to break,
And the light shoots like a streak
Of subtle fire; the wind blows cold,
Whilst the morning doth unfold;
Now the birds begin to rouse,
And the squirrel from the boughs
Leaps, to get him nuts and fruit:
The early lark, that erst was mute,
Carols to the rising day
Many a note and many a lay!

John Fletcher
(1579–1625)

To the lark

Good speed, for I this day
Betimes my matins say:
    Because I do
    Begin to woo,
    Sweet-singing lark,
    Be thou the clerk,
    And know thy when
    To say, Amen.
    And if I prove
    Bless'd in my love,
    Then shalt thou be
    High-priest to me,
    At my return,
    To incense burn;

And so to solemnise
Love's and my sacrifice.

Robert Herrick
(1591–1674)

To the morning lark

Feathered lyric! warbling high,
Sweetly gaining on the sky –
Opening with thy matin lay
Nature's hymn, the eye of day,
Teach my soul, on early wing,
Thus to soar, and thus to sing!

While the bloom of Orient light
Guides thee in thy tuneful flight,
May the day-spring from on high,
Seen by Faith's religious eye,
Cheer me with his vital ray,
Promise of eternal day!

Anon.
(17th Century)

The dead lark

Ah! there it falls, and now 'tis dead,
The shot went through its pretty head,
   And broke its shining wing!
How dull and dim its closing eyes!
How cold, and stiff, and still it lies,
   Poor harmless little thing!

It was a lark, and in the sky
In mornings fair it mounted high
   To sing a merry song;
Cutting the fresh and healthy air,
It whistled out its music there,
   As light it skimmed along.

All night beneath her pretty breast
She warmed her young ones in her nest,
   Hid in the springing corn;
And when she saw the sun arise,
She flew up singing to the skies,
   Ah, never to return!

Poor little bird! her helpless brood,
Who cry in vain for care or food,
   Will die when dark night lowers;
Nor shall we see her mounting wing,
Or hear her song that told of spring,
   And budding leaves, and flowers!

Anon.
(17th Century)

The lark

Swift through the yielding air I glide
While night's sable shades abide,
Yet in my flight, though ne'er so fast,
I tune and time the wild wind's blast;

And e'er the sun be come about
Teach the young lark her lesson out;
Who, early as the day is born,
Sings his shrill *Ave* to the rising morn.

Let never mortal lose the pain
To imitate my airy strain,
Whose pitch, too high for human ears,
Was set me by the tuneful spheres.

I carol to the faerie king,
Wake him a mornings when I sing,
And when the sun stoops to the deep,
Rock him again and his fair queen asleep.

Anon.
(before 1660)

Song

The lark now leaves his wat'ry nest
And climbing, shakes his dewy wings;
He takes this window for the east,
And to implore your light, he sings,
Awake, awake, the morn will never rise,
Till she can dress her beauty at your eyes.

The merchant bows unto the seaman's star,
The ploughman from the sun his season takes;
But still the lover wonders what they are,
Who look for day before his Mistress wakes,
Awake, awake, break through your veils of lawn!
Then draw your curtains, and begin the dawn.

Sir William D'Avenant
(1606–1668)

L'allegro

To hear the Lark begin his flight,
And singing startle the dull night,
From his watch-tower in the skies,
Till the dappled dawn doth rise;
Then to com in spight of sorrow,
And at my window bid good morrow,
Through the Sweet-Briar, or the Vine,
Or the twisted Eglantine,
While the cock with lively din,
Scatters the rear of darkness thin,
And to the stack or the Barn dore,
Stoutly struts his Dames before,
Oft list'ning how the Hounds and horn
Clearly rouse the slumbering Morn,
From the side of Som Hoar Hill,
Through the high wood echoing shrill
Som time walking not unseen
By Hedge-row Elms, on Hillocks green.
Right against the Eastern gate,
Wher the great Sun begins his state,

Rob'd in flames, and Amber light,
The clouds in thousand Liveries dight.
While the Plowman neer at hand,
Whistles o'er the Furrow'd Land,
And the Milkmaid singeth blithe,
And the Mower whets his sithe,
And every Shepherd tels his tale
Under the Hawthorn in the dale.

John Milton
(1608–1674)

from Ode X: The first of April

The swallow, for a moment seen,
Skims in haste the village green;
From the grey moor, on feeble wing,
The screaming plovers idly spring.
The butterfly, gay-painted soon,
Explores awhile the tepid moon;
And fondly trusts its tender dyes
To fickle suns and flattering skies.
Fraught with a transient, frozen shower,
If a cloud should haply lower,
Sailing o'er the landscape dark,
Mute on a sudden is the lark;
But when gleams the sun again
O'er the pearl-besprinkled plain,
And from behind his water veil
Looks through the thin descending hail;
She mounts, and lessening to the sight,
Salutes the blithe return of light,

And high her tuneful track pursues
Mid the dim rainbow's scattered hues.
Where in venerable rows
Widely waving oaks enclose
The moat of yonder antique hall,
Swarm the rooks with clamorous call;
And to the toils of nature true,
Wreathe their capacious nests anew.

John Milton

Upon the lark and the fowler

Thou simple bird what mak'st thou here to play?
Look, there's the Fowler, prethee come away.
Dost not behold the Net? Look there 'tis spread,
Venture a little further thou art dead.
Is there not room enough in all the Field
For thee to play in, but thou needs must yield
To the deceitful glitt'ring of a Glass,
Placed twixt Nets to bring thy death to pass?

Bird, if thou art so much for dazling light,
Look, there's the Sun above thee, dart upright.
Thy nature is to soar up to the Sky
Why wilt thou come down to the nets and dye?
Take no heed to the Fowler's tempting Call;
This whistle he enchanteth Birds withal.
Or if thou seest a live Bird in his net
Believe she's there 'cause thence she cannot get.
Look how he tempteth thee with his Decoy
That he may rob thee of thy Life, thy Joy:

40

Come, prethee, Bird, I prethee come away,
Why should this net thee take when 'scape thou may?
    Hadst thou not wings, or were thy feathers pulled,
Or wast thou blind, or fast asleep wer't lulled:
The case would somewhat alter, but for thee
Thy eyes are ope, and thou hast Wings to see.
    Remember that thy Song is in thy Rise,
Not in thy Fall, Earth's not thy Paradise.
Keep up aloft then, let thy circuits be
Above, where Birds from Fowlers nets are free....

    A skylark wounded in the wing,
    A cherubim does cease to sing.

John Bunyan
(1628–1688)

The lark

The giddy lark reacheth the steepy air
By sweet degrees, making each note a stair.
Her voice leads softly on, the feather'd strain
Follows, and leaves the last note to her train.
At the first stage she rests, seeming to tire;
Her wing mounts up her voice some eight notes higher.
At the next period in this airy hill,
Her rising voice lifts up her restive quill.
Hard tale to tell, when she her matins sings,
Whether her tongue gives, or receives her wings.
To the observing ear, attentive eye,
Her wings would seem to chant, her tongue to fly.

Brave flight of music, and a sublime song,
When wings thus sweetly fly into a tongue!
Throned on the welkin's crest, her voice the stair
Stills with her wings, and here becomes a chair:
Where seated, in a calm sweet strain she sings,
A loss to earth, without her tongue or wings.
She streams away in rapture, turned clear
Into a soft piece of harmonious air,
All sung into a jelly; now become
A nectar cloud, moved by a sphery tongue.
Lost to herself (poor bird!) as now to me
Who nothing but her air-strook voice might see.
But like a silver bell, that stands brim-full
Of its own sound, till the relenting pull
Shake off the pleasing trance: a broke note crossed
Put her marred wings in mind that she was lost.
Then (like the air that o'er the treble string
Trembleth its life away, soft hovering
Till by the base recalled) the liquid fowl
Strook solid, sings her body to her soul.
Lord! with what art she ruins in her fall,
As he that in division shuts up all:
Clad in a light held saraband, whose pace
Merrily winds her down to her first place.
Thus, as her body biggens, still her song
Draws near our sense, we understand her tongue.
But earth (as if resolved to interrupt
And rise amongst her numbers, now abrupt)
Gives her a dampy touch, that doth benumb
Her soul, and strikes her contemplation dumb.

Anon.
(17th Century)

The lark in the morn
Folk song

As I was a-walking
One morning in the spring,
I met a pretty maiden
So sweetly she did sing.
And as we were a-walking
These words she did say,
'There's no life like the ploughboy's
All in the month of May.

'The lark in the morn
She doth rise up from her nest,
And mounts upon the air
With the dew all on her breast.
And like the pretty ploughboy
She doth whistle and doth sing,
And at night she doth return
To her own nest back again.'

Anon.
(17th Century)

Daybreak

Daybreak –
On the corn shoots
White frost of spring.

It's summer; then
'Oh, let's have winter,'
Some men say.

43

Will there be any
Not wielding his brush?
The moon tonight.

To know the plums,
Own your heart
And own your nose.

Come, come, I say;
But the firefly
Goes on his way.

They bloom and then
We look and then they
Fall and then...

Trout leaping:
On the river-bed
Clouds floating.

Green cornfield:
A skylark soaring,
There – swooping.

Uejima Onitsura
(1661–1738)

The English ideal

In some small hamlet on the lonely plain,
Where Thames, thro' meadows, rolls his mazy train;
Or where high Windsor, thick with greens array'd,

Waves his old oaks, and spreads his ample shade,
Fancy has figur'd out our calm retreat;
Already round the visionary seat
Our limes begin to shoot, our flow'rs to spring,
The brooks to murmur, and the birds to sing.
Where dost thou lie, thou thinly-peopled green?
Thou nameless lawn, and village yet unseen?
Where sons, contented with their native ground,
Ne'er travell'd further than ten furlongs round;
And the tann'd peasant, and his ruddy bride,
Were born together, and together died.
Where early larks best tell the morning-light,
And only Philomel disturbs the night,
'Midst gardens here my humble pile shall rise,
With sweets surrounded of ten thousand dyes;
All savage where th'embroider'd gardens end,
The haunt of echoes shall my woods ascend;
And O! if heav'n th'ambitious thought approve,
A rill shall warble cross the gloomy grove,
A little rill, o'er pebbly beds convey'd,
Gush down the steep, and glitter thro' the glade.
What cheering scents those bord'ring banks exhale!
How loud that heifer lows from yonder vale!

Thomas Tickell
(1686–1740)

45

from **Essay on man**

Has God, thou fool! work'd solely for thy good,
Thy joy, thy pastime, thy attire, thy food?

Is it for thee the lark ascends and sings?
Joy tunes his voice, joy elevates his wings.

Is it for thee the linnet pours his throat?
Loves of his own and raptures swell the note.

Is thine alone the seed that strews the plain?
The birds of heaven shall vindicate their grain.

Alexander Pope
(1688–1744)

Prelude

...Up springs the lark,
Shrill-voiced. and loud, the messenger of morn;
Ere yet the shadows fly, he mounted sings
Amid the dawning clouds, and from their haunts
Calls up the tuneful nations. Every copse
Deep-tangled, tree irregular, and bush
Bending with dewy moisture, o'er the heads
Of the coy quiristers that lodge within,
Are prodigal of harmony. the thrush
And woodlark, o'er the kind-contending throng

Superior heard, run thro' the sweetest length
Of notes; when listening *Philomela* deigns
To let them joy, and purposes, in thought
Elate, to make her night exceed their day!

James Thomson
(1700–1748)

Song: The skylark

Go, tuneful bird, that glad'st the skies,
　　To Daphne's window speed thy way;
And there on quiv'ring pinions rise,
　　And there thy vocal art display.

And if she deign thy notes to hear,
　　And if she praise thy matin song,
Tell her, the sounds that soothe her ear,
　　To Damon's native plains belong.

Tell her, in livelier plumes array'd,
　　The bird from Indian groves may shine;
But ask the lovely partial maid
　　What are his notes compared to thine?

Then bid her treat yon witless beau
　　And all his flaunting race with scorn;
And lend an ear to Damon's woe,
　　Who sings her praise, and sings forlorn.

William Shenstone
(1714–1763)

from **Ode**
On the Pleasure arising from Vicissitude

Now the golden Morn aloft
Waves her dew-bespangled wing,
With vermil cheek, and whisper soft
She wooes the tardy Spring:
Till April starts, and calls around
The sleeping fragrance from the ground;
And lightly o'er the living scene
Scatters his freshest, tenderest green.

New-born flocks, in rustic dance,
Frisking ply their feeble feet;
Forgetful of their wintry trance
The birds his presence greet:
But chief, the Sky-Lark warbles high
His trembling thrilling extacy;
And, lessening from the dazzled sight,
Melts into air and liquid light.

Rise, my Soul! on wings of fire,
Rise the rapt'rous Choir among;
Hark! 'tis Nature strikes the Lyre,
And leads the general song:
Warm let the Lyric transport flow,
Warm as the ray that bids it glow;
And animates the vernal grove
With health, with harmony, and love...

Thomas Gray
(1718–1771)

48

The poet's arbour in the birch-wood

Gloomy am I, oppressed and sad; love is not for me while winter lasts, until May comes to make the hedges green with its green veil over every lovely greenwood. There I have got a merry dwelling-place, a green pride of green leaves, a bright joy to the heart, in the glade of dark green thick-grown pathways, well-rounded and trim, a pleasant paling. Odious men do not come there and make their dwellings, nor any but my deft gracious gentle-hearted love. Delightful is its aspect, snug when the leaves come, the green house on the lawn under its pure mantle. It has a fine porch of soft bushes; and on the ground green field clover. There the skilled cuckoo, amorous, entrancing, sings his pure song full of love-longing; and the young thrush in its clear mellow language sings glorious and bright, the gay poet of summer; the merry woodland nightingale plies incessantly in the green leaves its songs of love-making; and with the daybreak the lark's glad singing makes sweet verses in swift outpouring We shall have every joy of the sweet long day if I can bring you there for a while, my Gwenno.

Iolo Morgannwg
(1747–1827)

from The schoolboy

I love to rise in a summer morn,
When the birds sing on every tree;
The distant huntsman winds his horn,
And the skylark sings with me:
    O what sweet company!...

William Blake
(1757–1827)

49

Birdsong

Thou hearest the Nightingale begin the Song of Spring.
The Lark sitting upon his earthy bed, just as the morn
Appears, listens silent; then springing from the waving
    Cornfield, loud
He leads the Choir of Day: trill, trill, trill trill,
Mounting upon the wings of light into the Great Expanse,
Re-echoing against the lovely blue & shining heavenly Shell,
His little throat labours with inspiration; every feather
On throat & breast & wings vibrates with the effluence Divine.
All Nature listens silent to him, & the awful Sun
Stands still upon the mountain looking on this little Bird
With eyes of soft humility & wonder, love & awe,
Then loud from their green covert all the Birds begin their Song:
The Thrush, the Linnet & the Goldfinch, Robin & the Wren
Awake the Sun from his sweet reverie upon the mountain.
The Nightingale again assays his song, & thro' the day
And thro' the night warbles luxuriant, every Bird of Song
Attending his loud harmony with admiration & love.

William Blake

from **When the kye come hame**

    Come all ye jolly shepherds
      That whistle through the glen,
    I'll tell ye of a secret
      That courtiers dinna ken:
    What is the greatest bliss
      That the tongue o' man can name?
    'Tis to woo a bonnie lass

When the kye come hame.
   When the kye come hame,
     When the kye come hame,
     'Tween the gloamin' and the mirk,
     When the kye come hame.
'Tis not beneath the burgonet,
  Nor yet beneath the crown,
'Tis not on couch of velvet
  Nor yet on bed of down;
'Tis beneath the spreading birch,
  In the dell without a name,
Wi' a bonnie, bonnie lassie,
  When the kye come hame.
There the blackbird bigs his nest
  For the mate he loves to see,
And up upon the tapmost bough,
  Oh, a happy bird is he!
Then he pours his melting ditty,
  And love 'tis a' the theme,
And he'll woo his bonnie lassie
  When the kye come hame.
When the bluart bears a pearl,
  And the daisy turns a pea,
And the bonny lucken gowan
  Has fauldit up his e'e,
Then the laverock frae the blue lift
  Draps down, and thinks nae shame
To woo his bonnie lassie
  When the kye come hame...

Robert Burns
(1759–1796)

On tree or bush...

On tree or bush no lark was ever seen:
The daisied lea he loves, where tufts of grass
Luxuriant crown the ridge; there, with his mate,
He founds their lowly house, of withered bents,
And coarsest speargrass; next, the inner work
With finer and still finer fibres lays,
Rounding it curious with his speckled breast.

James Grahame
(1763–1811)

The skylark

BIRD of the wilderness,
Blithesome and cumberless,
Sweet by thy matin o'er moorland and lea!
Emblem of happiness,
Blest is thy dwelling-place,
O to abide in the desert with thee!
Wild is thy lay and loud,
Far in the downy cloud,
Loves gives it energy, love gave it birth,
Where, on thy dewy wing,
Where art thou journeying?
Thy lay is in heaven, thy love is on earth.

O'er fell and fountain sheen,
O'er moor and mountain green,
O'er the red streamer that heralds the day,
Over the cloudlet dim,

Over the rainbow's rim,
Musical cherub, soar, singing, away!
Then, when the gloaming comes,
Low in the heather blooms,
Sweet will thy welcome and bed of love be!
Emblem of happiness,
Blest is thy dwelling-place
O to abide in the desert with thee!

James Hogg
(1770–1835)

To the skylark

Ethereal Minstrel! Pilgrim of the sky!
Dost thou despise the earth where cares abound?
Or, while the wings aspire, are heart and eye
Both with thy nest upon the dewy ground?
Thy nest which thou canst drop into at will
Those quivering wings composed, that music still!

To the last point of vision, and beyond,
Mount, daring Warbler! That love-prompted strain,
('Twixt thee and thine a never-failing bond)
Thrills not the less the bosom of the plain.

Yet might'st thou seem, proud privilege! To sing
All independent of the leafy spring.

Leave to the Nightingale her shady wood,
A privacy of glorious light is thine,
Whence thou dost pour upon the world a flood

Of harmony, with instinct more divine,
Type of the wise who soar, but never roam,
True to the kindred points of Heaven and Home!

William Wordsworth
(1770–1850)

To a skylark

Up with me; up with me into the clouds!
  For thy song, Lark, is strong;
Up with me, up with me into the clouds;
      Singing, singing.
With clouds and sky about thee ringing,
  Lift me, guide me till I find
That spot which seems so to thy mind!
I have walked through wildernesses dreary
And to-day my heart is weary;
Had I now the wings of a Faery,
Up to thee would I fly.
There is madness about thee, and joy divine
In that song of thine;
Lift me, guide me high and high
To thy banqueting place in the sky.
      Joyous as morning
Thou art laughing and scorning;
Thou hast a nest for thy love and thy rest,
And, though little troubled with sloth,
Drunken Lark! thou would'st be loth
To be such a traveller as I.
Happy, happy Liver,
With a soul as strong as a mountain river

Pouring out praise to the Almighty Giver,
  Joy and jollity be with us both!
Alas! my journey, rugged and uneven,
Through prickly moors or dusty ways must wind;
But hearing thee, or others of thy kind,
As full of gladness and as free of heaven,
I, with my fate contented, will plod on.
And hope for higher raptures, when life's day is done.

William Wordsworth

The plea

Who can divine what impulses from God
Reach the caged lark within a town abode,
From his poor inch or two of daisied sod?
O yield him back his privilege! No sea
Swells like the bosom of a man set free;
A wilderness is rich with liberty:
Roll on ye spouting Whales, who die or keep
Your independence in the fathomless deep!
Spread, tiny Nautilus, the living sail;
Dive at thy choice; or brave the freshening gale!

William Wordsworth

from **Song of the dawn**

BIRDS of omen dark and foul,
Night-crow, raven, bat, and owl,
Leave the sick man to his dream –

All night long he heard your scream.
Haste to cave and ruin'd tower,
Ivy tod, or dingle-bower,
There to wink and mope, for, hark!
In the mild air sings the lark.

Sir Walter Scott
(1771–1832)

Answer to a child's question

Do you ask what the birds say? The sparrow, the dove,
The linnet and the thrush say "I love and I love!"
In the winter they're silent – the wind is so strong;
What it says I don't know, but it sings a loud song.
But green leaves and blossoms, and sunny warm weather,
And singing, and loving – all come back together.
But the lark is so brimful of gladness and love,
The green fields below him, the blue sky above,
That he sings, and he sings; and forever sings he –
'I love my Love, and my Love loves me!'

Samuel Taylor Coleridge
(1772–1834)

from The rime of the ancient mariner

Around, around, flew each sweet sound,
Then darted to the Sun;
Slowly the sounds came back again,
Now mixed, now one by one.

Sometimes a-dropping from the sky
I heard the skylark sing;
Sometimes all little birds that are,
How they seemed to fill the sea and air
With their sweet jargoning !

And now 'twas like all instruments,
Now like a lonely flute;
And now it is an angel's song,
That makes the heavens be mute.

It ceased; yet still the sails made on
A pleasant noise till noon,
A noise like of a hidden brook
In the leafy month of June,
That to the sleeping woods all night
Singeth a quiet tune.

Samuel Taylor Coleridge

On a picture by J. M. Wright, Esq
[Engraved for the Keepsake of 1829]

The sky-lark hath perceived his prison-door
 Unclosed; for liberty the captive tries:
Puss eagerly hath watched him from the floor,
 And in her grasp he flutters, pants, and dies.

Lucy's own Puss, and Lucy's own dear Bird,
 Her foster'd favourites both for many a day.
That which the tender-hearted girl preferr'd,
 She in her fondness knew not sooth to say.

57

For if the sky-lark's pipe were shrill and strong,
    And its rich tones the thrilling ear might please,
Yet Pussybel could breathe a fireside song
    As winning, when she lay on Lucy's knees.

Both knew her voice, and each alike would seek
    Her eye, her smile, her fondling touch to gain:
How faintly then may words her sorrow speak,
    When by the one she sees the other slain.

The flowers fall scatter'd from her lifted hands;
    A cry of grief she utters in affright;
And self-condemn'd for negligence she stands
    Aghast and helpless at the cruel sight.

Come, Lucy, let me dry those tearful eyes;
    Take thou, dear child, a lesson not unholy,
From one whom nature taught to moralize
    Both in his mirth and in his melancholy.

I will not warn thee not to set thy heart
    Too fondly upon perishable things;
In vain the earnest preacher spends his art
    Upon that theme; in vain the poet sings.

It is our nature's strong necessity,
    And this the soul's unerring instincts tell:
Therefore I say, let us love worthily,
    Dear child, and then we cannot love too well.

Better it is all losses to deplore,
    Which dutiful affection can sustain,
Than that the heart should, in its inmost core,
    Harden without it, and have lived in vain.

This love which thou hast lavish'd, and the woe
　　Which makes thy lip now quiver with distress,
Are but a vent, an innocent overflow,
　　From the deep springs of female tenderness.

And something I would teach thee from the grief
　　That thus hath fill'd those gentle eyes with tears,
The which may be thy sober, sure relief
　　When sorrow visits thee in after years.

I ask not whither is the spirit flown
　　That lit the eye which there in death is seal'd;
Our Father hath not made that mystery known;
　　Needless the knowledge, therefore not reveal'd.

But didst thou know in sure and sacred truth,
　　It had a place assign'd in yonder skies,
There through an endless life of joyous youth,
　　To warble in the bowers of Paradise;

Lucy, if then the power to thee were given
　　In that cold form its life to re-engage,
Wouldst thou call back the warbler from its Heaven,
　　To be again the tenant of a cage?

Only that thou might'st cherish it again,
　　Wouldst thou the object of thy love recall
To mortal life, and chance, and change, and pain,
　　And death, which must be suffered once by all?

Oh, no, thou say'st: oh, surely not, not so!
　　I read the answer which those looks express:
For pure and true affection well I know
　　Leaves in the heart no room for selfishness.

Such love of all our virtues is the gem;
  We bring with us the immortal seed at birth:
Of heaven it is, and heavenly; woe to them
  Who make it wholly earthly and of earth!

What we love perfectly, for its own sake
  We love and not our own, being ready thus
Whate'er self-sacrifice is ask'd, to make;
  That which is best for it, is best for us.

O Lucy! Treasure up that pious thought!
  It hath a balm for sorrow's deadliest darts;
And With true comfort thou wilt find it fraught,
  If grief should reach thee in thy heart of hearts.

Robert Southey
(1774–1843)

from **The bells of Fife**

The fair Earth laughs through all her boundless range,
  Heaving her green hills high to greet the beam;
City and village, steeple, cot and grange,
  Gilt as with nature's purest leaf-gold seem;
The heaths and upland muirs, and fallows, change
  Their barren brown into a ruddy gleam,
And, on ten thousand dew-bent leaves and sprays,
Twinkle ten thousand suns and fling their petty rays.

Up from their nests and fields of tender corn
  Full merrily the little sky-larks spring,
And on their dew-bedabbled pinions born,

60

Mount to the heav'n's blue key-stone flickering;
They turn their plume-soft bosoms to the morn,
  And hail the genial light and cheerly sing;
Echo the gladsome hills and valleys round,
And half the bells of Fife ring loud and swell the sound...

And, from our steeple's pinnacle outspread,
  The town's long colours flare and flap on high,
Whose anchor, blazoned fair in green and red,
  Curls, pliant to each breeze that whistles by;
Whilst on the boltsprit stern and topmast-head
  Of brig and sloop that in the harbour lie,
Streams the red gaudery of flags in air
All to salute and grace the morn of Anster Fair.

William Tennant
(1784–1848)

Skylark, bird of the bright infinity

I watched thee, lessening, lessening to the sight;
  Still faint and fainter winnowing
  The sunshine with thy dwindling wing,
A speck, a movement in the ruffled light;
  Till thou wert melted in the sky,
An undistinguish'd part of the bright infinity.

Meet emblem of that lightsome spirit, thou!
  That still, wherever it might come,
  Shed sunshine o'er that happy home.
Her task of kindliness and gladness now
  Absolved, with the element above
Hath mingled, and become pure light, pure joy, pure love.

Henry Hart Milman.
(1791–1868)

To a skylark

Hail to thee, blythe spirit!
  Bird thou never wert,
That from heaven, or near it,
  Pourest thy full heart
In profuse strains of unpremeditated art.

Higher still and higher
  From the earth thou springest
Like a cloud of fire;
  The blue deep thou wingest,
And singing still dost soar, and soaring ever singest.

In the golden lightning
    Of the sunken sun
O'er which clouds are brightening,
    Thou dost float and run,
Like an unbodied joy whose race is just begun.

The pale purple even
    Melts around thy flight;
Like a star of heaven,
    In the broad daylight
Thou art unseen, but yet I hear thy shrill delight:

Keen as are the arrows
    Of that silver sphere,
Whose intense lamp narrows
    In the white dawn clear
Until we hardly see, we feel that it is there.

All the earth and air
    With thy voice is loud,
As, when night is bare,
    From one lonely cloud
The moon rains out her beams, and heaven is overflow'd.

What thou art we know not;
    What is most like thee?
From rainbow clouds there flow not
    Drops so bright to see,
As from thy presence showers a rain of melody.

Like a poet hidden
    In the light of thought,
Singing hymns unbidden,
    Till the world is wrought
To sympathy with hopes and fears it heeded not:

Like a high-born maiden
    In a palace tower,
Soothing her love-laden
    Soul in secret hour
With music sweet as love, which overflows her bower:

Like a glow-worm golden
    In a fall of dew,
Scattering unbeholden
    Its aerial hue
Among the flowers and grass, which screen it from the view;

Like a rose embowered
    In its own green leaves,
By warm winds deflower'd,
    Till the scent it gives
Makes faint with too much sweet these heavy-wingèd thieves.

Sound of vernal showers
    On the twinkling grass,
Rain-awakened flowers –
    All that ever was
Joyous, and clear, and fresh, thy music doth surpass.

Teach us, sprite or bird,
    What sweet thoughts are thine:
I have never heard,
    Praise of love or wine
That panted forth a rapture so divine.

Chorus hymeneal,
    Or triumphal chant,
Matched with thine would be all
    But an empty vaunt,
A thing therein we feel there is some hidden want.

What objects are the fountains
    Of thy happy strain?
What fields, or waves, or mountains?
    What shapes of sky or plain?
What love of thine own kind? what ignorance of pain.

With thy clear keen joyance
    Languor cannot be,
Shadow of annoyance
    Never came near thee:
Thou lovest – but ne'er knew love's sad satiety.

Waking or asleep,
    Thou of death must deem
Things more true and deep
    Than we mortals dream,
Or how could thy notes flow in such a crystal stream?

We look before and after,
And pine for what is not;
Our sincerest laughter
With some pain is fraught;
Our sweetest songs are those that tell of saddest thought.

Yet, if we could scorn
Hate, and pride, and fear,
If we were things born
Not to shed a tear,
I know not how thy joy we ever should come near.

Better than all measures
Of delightful sound,
Better than all treasures
That in books are found,
Thy skill to poet were, thou scorner of the ground!

Teach me half the gladness
That thy brain must know,
Such harmonious madness
From my lips would flow,
The world should listen then, as I am listening now!

Percy Bysshe Shelley
(1792–1822)

The lark's nest

From yon black clump of wheat that grows
More rank and higher than the rest,
A lark – I marked her as she rose –

At early morning left her nest.
Her eggs were four of dusky hue,
Blotched brown as is the ground,
With tinges of a purple hue
The larger ends encircling round.

Behind a clod how snug the nest
Is in a horse's footing fixed!
Of twitch and stubbles roughly dressed,
With roots and horsehair intermixed.
The wheat surrounds it like a bower,
And like to thatch each bowing blade
T'grows off the frequent falling shower
– And here's an egg this morning laid!

John Clare
(1793–1864)

Spearthistle

...Where the broad sheepwalk bare and brown
        Yields scant grass pining after showers,
And winds go fanning up and down
        The little strawy bents and nodding flowers,
There the huge thistle, spurred with many thorns,
The suncrackt upland's russet swells adorns...

The horse will set his foot and bite
        Close to the ground lark's guarded nest
And snort to meet the prickly sight;
He fans the feathers of her breast-

Yet thistles prick so deep that he
Turns back and leaves her dwelling free.

John Clare

Larks and spring

The sunny end of March is nigh
And not a cloud is in the sky
Along the footpath o'er the farm
The school-boy basket on his arm
Seeks the bird's nest therein to look
He takes a stone to cross the brook
Made wider by the rainy night
And hums the music of delight
To see the rabits seek their burrow
Or ground lark from the fallow'd furrow
Start up and shiver while he sings
Then drop as though he'd lost his wings
As stunt and heavy as a stone
In the brown furrow still and lone
And still I love the ground-lark's flight
Starting up the ploughman's height
And more and more unseal his eye
To see the skylark as he springs
Shake morning's moisture from his wings
And rise and sing in music proud
Small as a bee beneath a cloud
'Till mixing with the vapours dun
He's lost in valleys of the sun
And singing on in spring's delight
Some moments e're he comes in sight

It drops, and droops from breezy morn
To seek its mate amid the corn
A happy song the skylark brings
And spring's in every note he sings
With coppled crown and speckled breast
The pilewort blooms above his nest
In rain it seeks the sheltering furrow
But sings when sunshine comes tomorrow
In every field they mount and sing
The song of Nature and of Spring

John Clare

The sky lark leaving her nest

Right happy bird so full of mirth
Mounting and mounting still more high
To meet morns sunshine in the sky
Ere yet it smiles on earth

How often I delight to stand
Listening a minute's length away
Where summer spreads her green array
By wheat or barley land

To see thee with a sudden start
The green and placid herbage leave
And in mid air a vision weave
For joys delighted heart

Shedding to heaven a vagrant mirth
When silence husheth other themes

And woods in their dark splendour dreams
Like heaviness on earth

My mind enjoys the happy sight
To watch thee to the clear blue sky
And when I downward turn my eye
Earth glows with lonely light

Then nearer comes thy happy sounds
And downward drops thy little wing
And now the valleys hear thee sing
And all the dewy grounds

Gleam into joy now from the eye
Thou'rt dropping sudden as a stone
And now thour't in the wheat alone
And still the circle of the sky

And abscent like a pleasure gone
Though many come within the way
Thy little song to peeping day
Is still remembered on

For who that crosses fields of corn
Where sky larks start to meet the day
But feels more pleasure on his way
Upon a summers morn

'Tis one of those heart cheering sights
In green earths rural chronicles
That upon every memory dwells
Among home fed delights

John Clare

70

To the lark

Bird of the morn,
When roseate clouds begin
To show the opening dawn,
Thy singing does begin,
And o'er the sweet green fields and happy vales
Thy pleasant song is heard, mixed with the morning gales.

Bird of the morn,
What time the ruddy sun
Smiles on the pleasant corn
Thy singing is begun,
Heartfelt and cheering over labourers' toil,
Who chop in coppice wild and delve the russet soil.

Bird of the sun,
How beautiful art thou!
When morning has begun
To gild the mountain's brow,
How beautiful it is to see thee soar so blest,
Winnowing thy russet wings above thy twitchy nest.

Bird of the summer's day,
How oft I stand to hear
Thee sing thy airy lay,
With music wild and clear,
Till thou become a speck upon the sky,
Small as the clods that crumble where I lie.

Thou bird of happiest song,
The spring and summer too
Are thine, the months along,
The woods and vales to view.
If climes were evergreen thy song would be
The sunny music of eternal glee.

John Clare

from **Sonnet to Charles Wells**

'As late I rambled in the happy fields,
What time the skylark shakes the tremulous dew
From the lush clover covert,'...

John Keats
(1795–1821)

from **'Nepenthe'**

...Raising me on ethereal wing
Lighter than the lark can spring
When drunk with dewlight, which the Morn
Pours from her translucent horn
To steep his sweet throat in the corn...

George Darley
(1795–1846)

Heart of Midlothian

MOST lovely was the verdure of the hills –
A rich, luxuriant green, o'er which the sky
Of blue, translucent, clear without a cloud,
Outspread its arching amplitude serene.
With many a gush of music, from each brake
Sang forth the choral linnets; and the lark,
Ascending from the clover field, by fits
Soared as it sang, and dwindled from the sight.
The cushat stood amidst the topmost boughs
Of the tall tree, his white-ringed neck aslant,
Down thro' the leaves to see his brooding mate.
'Mid the tall meadow-grass the ox reclined,
Or bent his knee, or from beneath the shade
Of the broad beech, with ruminant mouth, gazed forth.
Rustling with wealth, a tissue of fair fields
Outstretched to left and right in luxury;
And the fir forests on the upland slopes
Contrasted darkly with the golden grain.

David Macbeth Moir
(1798–1851)

The lay of the lark

With dew upon its breast
   And sunshine on its wing,
The lark uprose from its happy nest,
   And thus it seemed to sing: –
'Sweet, sweet! from the middle of the wheat
   To meet the morning grey,
To leave the corn on a merry morn,
   Nor have to curse the day.'

With the dew upon their breast,
   And the sunlight on their wing,
Towards the skies from the furrows rise
   The larks, and thus they sing: –
'If you would know the cause
   That makes us sing so gay,
It is because we hail and bless,
   And never curse the day.'

Sweet, sweet! from the middle of the wheat
   (Where lurk our callow brood.)
Where we were hatch'd, and fed
Amidst the corn on a very merry morn,
   (We never starve for food.)
We never starve for bread!'
   •   •   •   •

Those flowers so very blue
　　Those poppies flaming red,
　·　　·　　·　　·

His heavy eye was glazed and dull,
　　He only murmur'd 'bread!'

Thomas Hood
(1799–1845)

Basque peasant returning from church

O little lark you need not fly
To seek your Master in the sky-
He treads our native sod.
Why should you sing aloft, apart?
Sing to the heaven of my heart
In me, in me, in me is God!

O stranger passing in your car,
You pity me who comes so far
On dusty feet, ill shod;
You cannot guess, you cannot know
Upon what wings of joy I go
Who travel home with God.

From far-off lands they bring your fare,
Earth's choicest morsels are your share,
And prize of gun and rod;
At richer boards I take my seat,
Have dainties angels may not eat;
In me, in me, in me is God !

O little lark sing loud and long
To Him who gave you flight and song
And me a heart aflame.
He loveth them of low degree
And He hath magnifièd me,
And holy, holy is His Name.

Anon.
(19th Century)

The lark

I am the sun's emissary,
Over whose monastic tower,
No doves of homage hover;
No rose of reverence grows.
Hence I go, ferried by devotion,
Under green rafters, or the eaves
Of strawberry leaves,
And eavesdrop in the wainscot of the world;
By trefoil bastioned; by sage and hellebore:
Where roots and sap connive and talk,
And the air of rustic lovers,
Goes sinewed with the plough's melodious walk.

Oh happy I!
On nest of threaded summers thus to lie;
Drinking the dew of nymphs' and shepherds' tales;
Stroking the faun-like legends as they fly;
While floating deep within my heart's quiet skies,
Yet lonely as a bucket in a well,
My starveling peer awaits,

And clangs his need impatient on my breast.
His burnished boredom shared alone with Time
(That deafest mute who only stares and stares),
Hindered by light from visualizing light;
While hells of ignorance go eagling through his brain.
Oh happy happy I!
In nest of goodly service thus to lie,
And know my lord's athirst for my warm word;
Sweet gossip for his unenlightened ear, –
I sleep, while night
Allows my dreams to steal her notes,
To twine moon music in my daily chimes.
Then morning tugs the bell rope of my throat,
Tossing me skywards, on rhapsodic wing,
And all my soul lichened with loveliness,
I give my lord his reverence – I sing.

Margaret Howard
(19th Century)

The gift

You heavens proud above this earth,
    Have you no shade but blue?
Your flow'ring stars are all alike,
    But gold and silver hue:
Your sun but one big iris-flower,
Your clouds are fair but pass in shower:
Live there in your huge sky
The hedge-rose or the campion
    Or purple dragon-fly?

Poor beggar sky! to you we'll send
  Out of our earthly store,
Out of our thousand, thousand sights
  And then a million more,
From all our shapes and colours fine,
From all our unthrift beauty's mine,
  A crumb from all our feast,
A gem from all our treasury,
The lark – our best and least.

Anon.
(19th Century)

The daisy

Now listen! In the country close by the high-road stood a farm-house: perhaps you have passed by and seen it for yourself. There was a little flower-garden with wooden palings: close by was a ditch and on its fresh green bank a daisy grew, and the sun shone as warmly on it as on the glorious flowers in the garden flower-beds, so the daisy did not mind being a poor despised flower, and turned towards the sun, and listened to the song of the skylark far above.

It was Monday, and the children were sitting on the forms at school, but the daisy was as happy as if the bright morning were a holiday for all, as she sat in the grass learning of the goodness of God, and rejoicing in the wild trilling song of the bird.

In the little garden were fine tulips and peonies: the daisy was so thankful that she could see their splendour through the palings. The lark suddenly flew down, down, not far from her, his song seeming louder and louder yet growing less and less. He ran at first a little way, unseen, through the grass, and then stopped, – not by the coloured garden flowers, but at the foot of the daisy herself. He danced round the lovely flower, singing again, and crying 'How beautiful is this soft green bank, How fair this simple flower with her golden heart and silver rays!' Then the daisy was happier than ever for she had always reverenced the singing bird. He kissed her, and took a bead of dew and rose again in full song.

Before the daisy closed her petals for the night a girl came into the garden with a sharp, shining knife and cut off some of the proud tulips, and even a peony. The daisy grieved for them; but her dreams were of the skylark's kiss.

Early next morning the bird was singing again but Oh such a mournful song, for it was caught, and in a tiny cage outside a window of the farm-house. The daisy longed to help her friend and the singing pierced her heart.

In a little while two boys came, and one had the bright knife that had cut the tulips off. They carved a square in the grass, leaving the daisy in the centre. 'Pull off the daisy' said one boy. 'No, leave it' replied the other, 'it looks so pretty.' Then they put the sod into the cage. The lark, remembering the daisy with joy, thrust his beak into the sod, for he had no water, and fire and ice seemed to consume his throat. Then he sipped the last drop of dew from the daisy's heart:

(but this, in reality, was a tear). He tried to sing to her, and opening his wings fluttered against the wires in anguish: soon, his heart, being broken, ceased to beat.

The boys wept when they found the lark had died, and buried it with full honours, in a little red box. The daisy they threw out in the dusty highway to die.

Hans Christian Andersen
(1805–1875)

The skylark

How blithe the lark runs up the golden stair
That leans through cloudy gates from heaven to earth,
And all alone in the empyreal air
Fills it with jubilant sweet songs of mirth!
How far he seems, how far
With the light upon his wings!
Is it a bird, or star
That shines, and sings?

What matter if the days be dark and frore,
That sunbeam tells of other days to be,
And singing in the light that floods him o'er
In joy he overtakes Futurity;
Under cloud-arches vast
He peeps, and sees behind
Great Summer coming fast
Adown the wind!

Frederick Tennyson
(1807–1898)

from **The gardener's daughter**

...From the woods
Came voices of the well-contented doves.
The lark could scarce get out his notes for joy,
But shook his song together as he near'd
His happy home, the ground.

Alfred, Lord Tennyson
(1809–1892)

The skylark *(Alauda arvensis)*

Upper parts reddish brown, the centre of each feather dark brown; a faint whitish streak above the eyes; throat white; neck and breast whitish, tinged with yellow and red, and streaked with dark brown; tail moderate. Length seven inches and a quarter. Eggs greyish, thickly speckled with dark grey and brown. A resident, breeding throughout the British Isles; also a passage migrant and winter visitor.

The Skylark, a bird whose flight and song are better known perhaps than those of any other bird, needs but a simple biography. The favourite bird of the poets, its story might be told in extracts compiled from various authors whose muse has led them to sing of Nature. Much, however, that has been written is but an amplification of the golden line, 'Hark, the Lark at Heaven's gate sings!' and not a little is an exaggerated statement of the height to which it ascends, and the time which it remains suspended in mid-air. But the Skylark needs no panegyrists, so, with all due deference to those who have struck the lyre in its honour, I will endeavour to describe its habits and haunts in humble prose.

The Skylark is a generally diffused bird, adapted by the conformation of its claws for perching on the ground, and by its length and power of wing for soaring high in the air. Accordingly, its food consists of small insects and seeds, which it collects among the herbage of stubble-fields, meadows and downs, or in newly ploughed fields. To this fare, it adds in winter and spring the tender stalks of' sprouting corn. Hence it is regarded with deadly hostility by farmers, and hence, too, the quiet of the country used to be much disturbed at these seasons by boys employed to frighten it away by screaming and plying a peculiar kind of rattle. During autumn and winter, Larks congregate in large flocks, and occupy their time principally in searching for food on the ground. If disturbed, they rise in a scattered manner, wheel about in the air until the flock is formed again, chirping from time to time, and then withdraw, not in a compact body, but at unequal distances from the earth and from each other, to a new feeding-ground, over which they hover with circling flight for some time before alighting. On trees they never perch; though one or two may occasionally be seen settled on a quickset hedge or a railing. In North Britain, at the approach of severe weather, they flock together and migrate southwards. Great numbers also visit England from the Continent, arriving in November, when they used to be caught in nets and traps for the table. Early in spring the flocks break up, when the birds pair, and for three or four months, every day and all day long, when the weather is fine (for the Lark dislikes rain and high winds), its song may be heard throughout the breadth of the land. Rising as it were by a sudden impulse from its nest or lowly retreat, it bursts forth, while as yet but a few feet from the ground, into exuberant song, and with its head turned towards the breeze, now ascending perpendicularly, and now veering to the right or left, but not describing circles, it pours forth an unbroken chain of melody, until it has reached an elevation computed to be, at the most, about a thousand feet. To an observer on earth, it has dwindled to the size of a mere speck; but, as far as my experience goes, it never rises so high as to defy the search of a keen eye. Having reached its highest elevation, its ambition is satisfied without making any permanent stay, and it begins to descend, not with a uniform downward motion, but by a series of droppings with intervals of simple hovering, during which it seems to be resting on its wings. Finally, as it draws near the earth, it ceases its song and descends more rapidly, but before it touches the ground it recovers itself, sweeps away with almost horizontal flight for a short distance and disappears in the herbage. The time consumed in this evolution is at the most from fifteen to twenty minutes, more frequently less; nor have I ever observed it partially descend and soar upwards again. A writer in the *Magazine of Natural History* maintains that 'those acquainted with the song of the Skylark, can tell, without looking at them, whether the birds be ascending or stationary in the air, or on their descent; so different is the style of the song in each case'. Mr. Yarrell is of the same opinion, and I have little doubt that they are correct, though I am not certain that I have myself attained the skill of discriminating. In July, the Lark ceases its soarings and song together, but in fine weather, in October, it receives a new inspiration and is musical again. From time to time, during winter, if the season be mild, it resumes its aerial habits, but it neither ascends so high nor sings so long, two or three minutes becoming now the limits of its performance. Like most other birds, it sings least about noon and the first two hours of the afternoon; but it begins before sunrise, having been heard at midsummer as early as two o'clock in the morning, and it sometimes continues its song till late on into the night, having been heard at ten o'clock when it was quite dark. Occasionally, too, it sings on the ground; and, in a cage, as all the world knows, it pours out its melody with as much spirit, as if its six inches of turf could be measured by acres, and the roof of its little cage were the vault of heaven. The following stanza in French is equally successful in imitating the song of the Skylark and describing its evolutions:

La gentille Alouette avec son tirelire,
Tirelire, relire et tirelirant, tire
Vers la voûte du ciel; puis son vol en ce lieu
Vire, et semble nous dire: Adieu, adieu, adieu.

The Lark builds its nest in a hollow in the ground, the rut of a cart-wheel, the depression formed by a horse's hoof, or in a hole which it scrapes out for itself. The nest is composed of dry grass, and lined with finer fibres. It lays four or five eggs, and rears two broods in the year. It displays great attachment to its young, and has been known, when disturbed by mowers, to build a dome over its nest, as a substitute for the natural shelter afforded by the grass while standing, and to remove its young in its claws to another place of concealment. In a cage, even the male is an excellent nurse. Mr. Weir mentions one which brought up several broods entrusted to its care, and a similar instance has fallen under my own notice. Larks frequently become the prey of the Hobby and Merlin, which pounce on them as they are on the point of leaving the ground, and bear them off with as much ease as they would a feather. But if an intended victim discovers its oppressor in time, it instantly begins to ascend with a rapidity which the other cannot follow, carried on as it is by the impetus of its horizontal flight. The Hawk, foiled for this time, renews the chase and endeavours to soar above its quarry; if it succeeds, it makes a second swoop, sometimes with deadly effect; but if it fails a second time, the Lark folds its wings, drops like lead to the ground, and, crouching among the herbage, often escapes detection.

Rev'd Charles Alexander Johns, F.L.S.
(1811–1874)

Nature smiles again

...for Nature, far above the evil passions of men, soon recovered Her serenity, and smiled upon the guilty battle-ground as she had done before, when it was innocent. The larks sang high above it; the swallows skimmed and dipped, and flitted to and fro; the shadows of the flying clouds pursued each other swiftly, over grass and corn and turnip-field and wood, and over roof, and church-spire in the nestling town among the trees away into the bright distance on the borders of the sky and earth, where the red sunsets faded. Crops were sown, and grew up, and were gathered in; the stream that had been crimsoned, turned a water-mill; men whistled at the plough; gleaners and haymakers were seen in quiet groups at work; sheep and oxen pastured; boys whooped and called, in fields, to scare away the birds; smoke rose from cottage chimneys; sabbath bells rang peacefully; old people lived and died; the timid creatures of the fields, and simple flowers of the bush and garden grew and withered in their destined terms.

Charles Dickens
(1812–1870)

85

Pippa passes

The year's at the spring
And day's at the morn;
Morning's at seven;
The hill-side's dew-pearled;
The lark's on the wing;
The snail's on the thorn;
God's in his heaven –
All's right with the world!

Robert Browning
(1812–1889)

The moors in summer

from *Wuthering Heights*

We planned where we would go, and what we would do in the summer... He said the pleasantest manner of spending a hot July day was lying from morning till evening on a bank of heather in the middle of the moors, with the bees humming dreamily about the bloom, and the larks singing high up over head, and the blue sky and bright sun shining steadily and cloudlessly. That was his most perfect idea of heaven's happiness: mine was rocking in a rustling green tree, with a west wind blowing, and bright white clouds flitting rapidly above; and not only larks, but throstles, and blackbirds and linnets, and cuckoos pouring out music on every side, and the moors seen at a distance, broken into cool dusky dells; but close by great swells of long grass undulating in waves to the breeze; and woods and sounding water, and the whole world awake and wild with joy. He wanted all to lie in an ecstasy of peace; I wanted all to sparkle and dance in a glorious jubilee. I said his heaven would be only half alive; and he said mine would be drunk: I said I should fall asleep in his; and he said he could not breathe in mine.

Emily Brontë
(1818–1848)

Like as the lark

Quale allodetta che in aere si spazia
Prima cantando, e poi tace, contenta,
Dell' ultima dolcezza che la sazia.
DANTE: *Paradiso, XX.*

Like as the lark that, soaring higher and higher,
Singeth awhile, then stops as't were content
   With his last sweetness, having filled desire,
So paused our bard; not for his force was spent,
   Nor that a string was loosened in his lyre,
But, having said his best and done his best,
   He could not better what was given before,
And threescore years and ten, demanding rest,
   Whispered, *They want thee on the other shore!*
And now he walks amid the learned throng,
   Haply with him who was the sixth of those
Who towered above the multitude in song,
   Or by the side of Geoffrey Chaucer goes,
Who shall remember with his wonted smile
How James found music in his antique style.

But we'll not mingle fancies with our sorrow
Nor from his own imagination borrow;
Holmes, who is left us best could speak his praise
Who knew his heart so well and loved his lays,
And whom Heaven crowns with greater length of days.

Thomas William Parsons
(1819–1892)

from **Inactivity**

I gave a moment to encase my books,
And I was in the sunshine, and my blood
Sprang at its greeting. I was in the fields,
And up around me sprang the larks like rockets
On a jubilee day: - a bank of sand surmounting,
I stepp'd into a wood, with pleasant care,
Opening the twining branches, that imposed
Desirable hindrance: angrily scream'd
A swiftly darting throstle on before me;
Two bees adown the narrow pathway flew,
And a bewilder'd butterfly; I stay'd
To joy in the delicious noise of leaves,
In the fresh earthy smells; - I wander'd on
Past the slow-pacing pheasant, and the jay,
Who would not let me leave him, but still follow'd
With his harsh scream. And now I reach'd an opening,
A short-turf'd lawn , that fenced by silvery stems
Of circling beeches, seem'd a quiet home.

I enter'd; flowingly between the trees
Floated the blackbird's strains; they paused, I paused;
Raising in sympathy to the tranquil heaven
My tranquil thought; like a great eye it shone,
It seem'd to bend in love; I gazed, and gazed;
Its look sank nearer me; I gasp'd, I fell,
Panting to be embraced up by the heaven,
As virgin womanhood for love's caress;
My soul close clung to that far-stretching glory,
'Neath which I reel'd; it stretch'd there undisturb'd
By tower or boundary, and my tranced spirit
Passively drank in its elysian calm.
Oh, blue, blue sky! oh fathomlessly blue sky!
Your motionless band of silvery cloudlets,
Like white swans sleeping on a windless lake,
In happy undesiring repose, - were not
More compass'd by you, more retired within you,
Than I, in that blest time; nor wish, nor thought,
Nor hope, nor grief, found room within my being,
Fill'd with your beautiful presence.

Within the sanctuary of these circling trees,
Thus lay I, slave to the sky; when a white deer
Noiselessly through the intertangled boughs
Did thrust his head; he shrank, and in the forest
Back vanished, most like a silvery cloud.
Retreating, he had shaken on my face
A blown convolvulus; the which upholding
Against the sun, that I might read its veins,
From its recess a crimson-scaled wonder,
A ladybird with richly-spotted wings,
Soar'd through the sunshine. Now from heaven's thraldom
My mind this insect's flight enfranchised;

And being freed to all the things around,
They all impress'd me. Now I heard the partridge
Make the copse echo with his cheerful crow;
Anon my pulsings seem'd to keep the time
Of the cuckoo's music; in the sun's faint streamings.
I watch'd the twinkling bands of tipsy insects;
I watch'd the sun's gold lustre through the leaves,
Illuminating all their make, descend,
As the breeze swerved them into it for a moment,
Letting them drop again. A hundred beauties,
Words will not image, throng'd my echoing soul
And she from all instinctively did abstract
Their capital feature; life, a massive lyre,
On my proud thought-directed vision rose,
Swinging within its home of boundlessness,
Singing for ever in an Eternal Breeze,
Of whom this landscape, with its gentle beauty,
Was one soft utterance....

Ebenezer Jones
(1820–1860)

Poem

A cloudless sky; a world of heather
Purple of foxglove; yellow of broom;
We two among it, wading together;
Shaking out honey, treading perfume.
Crowds of bees are giddy with clover,
Crowds of grasshoppers skip at our feet,
Crowds of larks at their matins hang over,
Thanking the Lord for a life so sweet.

Jean Ingelow
(1820–1897)

The bunch of larks

Portly he was, in carriage somewhat grand;
  Of gentleman he wore the accepted marks:
He thrid the busy street, and in his hand
  He bore a bunch of larks!

There be some things that may be carried – yes,
  A gentleman may carry larks – if dead;
Or any slaughtered game; not fish, still less
  The homely beef or bread.

I met him in the street, and turned about,
  And mused long after he had flaunted by.
A bunch of larks! and his intent, no doubt,
  To have them in a pie.

Yes, four-and-twenty larks baked in a pie!
  O, what a feast of melody is there!
The ringing chorus of a summer sky!
  A dish of warbling air!

How many dusty wanderers of the earth
  Have those stilled voices lifted from the dust!
And now to end their almost Heavenly mirth
  Beneath a gourmand's crust!

But as he picks their thin ambrosial throats,
  Will no accusing memories arise,
Of grassy glebes, and heaven-descending notes,
  And soul-engulfing skies?

'Give me,' cried he, 'the substance of the thing –
Something that I can eat, or drink, or feel –
A poem for the money it will bring –
Larks for a dainty meal.'

Well, he may have his substance, and I mine.
Deep in my soul the throbbing lark-notes lie.
My substance lasts, and takes a life divine –
His passes with the pie.

Robert Leighton
(1822–1869)

Tamerton church tower

In love with home, I rove tired eyed
The rainy North; but there
The distant hill-top in its pride,
Adorn'd the brilliant air;

And as I passed from Tavistock,
The scatter'd dwellings white,
The church, the golden weather-cock
Were whelm'd in hazy light;

Dark rocks shone forth with yellow brooms;
And, over orchard walls,
Gleam'd congregated apple-blooms,
In white and ruddy balls;

The children did the good sun greet,
  With song and senseless shout;
The lambs did skip, their dams did bleat,
  In Tavy leapt the trout,

Across the fleeting eastern cloud,
  The splendid rainbow sprang,
And larks, invisible and loud,
  Within its zenith sang.

Coventry Patmore
(1823–1896)

The lover and the birds

Within a budding grove
In April's ear sang every bird his best,
But not a song to pleasure my unrest
Or touch the tears unwept of bitter love;
Some spake, methought, with pity, some as if in jest:
  To every word
  Of every bird
I listen'd, and replied as it behove.

Scream'd Chaffinch, 'Sweet, sweet, sweet!
Pretty lovey, come and meet me here!'
'Chaffinch,' quoth I, 'be dumb awhile, in fear
Thy darling prove no better than a cheat,
And never come, or fly when wintry days appear.'
  Yet from a twig
  With voice so big
The little fowl his utterance did repeat.

93

Then I, 'The man forlorn
Hears Earth send up a foolish noise aloft.'
 – 'And what'll *he* do? What'll *he* do?' scoff'd
The Blackbird, standing in an ancient thorn,
Then spread his sooty wings and flitted to the croft
  With cackling laugh:
  Whom I, being half
Enraged, called after, giving back his scorn.

Worse mock'd the Thrush, 'Die! die!
Oh, could he do it? could he do it? Nay!
'Be quick! be quick! Here, here, here!' (went his lay)
'Take heed! take heed!' then, 'Why? why? why? why? why?
See-ee now! see-ee now!' (he drawled) 'Back! back! back!
        R-r-r-run away!'
  O thrush, be still!
  Or at thy will
Seek some less sad interpreter than I.

'Air, air! Blue air and white!
Whither I flee, whither, O whither, O whither I flee!'
(Thus the Lark hurried, mounting from the lea)
'Hills, countries, many waters glittering bright,
Whither I see, whither I see! deeper, deeper, deeper, whither
        I see, see, see!'
  'Gay Lark,' I said,
  'The song that's bred
In happy nest may well to heaven make flight.'

'There's something, something sad
I half remember' – piped a broken strain.
Well sung, sweet Robin! Robin sung again:
'Spring's opening, cheerily, cheerily! be we glad!'
Which moved, I wist not why, me melancholy mad,
   Till now, grown meek,
   With wetted cheek,
Most comforting and gentle thoughts I had.

William Allingham
(1824–1889)

The lark ascending

He rises and begins to round,
He drops the silver chain of sound,
Of many links without a break,
In chirrup, whistle, slur and shake,
All intervolved and spreading wide,
Like water-dimples down a tide
Where ripple ripple overcurls
And eddy into eddy whirls;
A press of hurried notes that run
So fleet they scarce are more than one,
Yet changeingly the trills repeat
And linger ringing while they fleet,
Sweet to the quick o' the ear, and dear
To her beyond the hand maid ear,
Who sits beside our inner springs,
Too often dry for this he brings,
Which seems the very jet of earth
At sight of sun, her music's mirth,

As up he winds the spiral stair,
A song of light, and pierces air
With fountain ardour, fountain play,
To reach the shining tops of day,
And drink in everything discerned
An ecstasy to music turned,
Impelled by what his happy bill
Disperses; drinking, showering still,
Unthinking save that he may give
His voice the outlet, there to live
Renewed in endless notes of glee,
So thirsty of his voice is he,
For all to hear and all to know
That he is joy, awake, aglow,
The tumult of the heart to hear
Through pureness filtered crystal-clear,
And know the pleasure sprinkled bright
By simple singing of delight,
Shrill, irreflective, unrestrained,
Rapt, ringing, on the jet sustained,
Without a break, without a fall,
Sweet silvery, sheer lyrical,
Perennial, quavering up the chord
Like myriad dews of sunny sward
That trembling into fulness shine,
And sparkle dropping argentine.

George Meredith
(1828–1909)

This poem provided the inspiration for
Ralph Vaughan Williams' 'The Lark Ascending':
a Romance for Violin and Orchestra *(Ed.)*.

A green cornfield

The earth was green, the sky was blue:
  I saw and heard one sunny morn
A skylark hang between the two,
  A singing speck above the corn;

A stage below, in gay accord,
  White butterflies danced on the wing,
And still the singing skylark soared,
  And silent sank and soared to sing.

The cornfield stretched a tender green
  To right and left beside my walks;
I knew he had a nest unseen
  Somewhere among the million stalks.

And as I paused to hear his song
  While swift the sunny moments slid,
Perhaps his mate sat listening long,
  And listened longer than I did.

Christina Rossetti
(1830–1894)

from **Summer**

…Summer days for me
When every leaf is on its tree;
When Robin's not a beggar,
And Jenny Wren's a bride,
And larks hang singing singing singing
Over the wheat fields wide –

Christina Rossetti

Poet and lark

When leaves turn outward to the light,
  And all the roads are fringed with green,
When larks are pouring, high, unseen,
  The joy they find in song and flight,
Then I, too, with the lark would wing
My little flight, and, soaring, sing.

When larks drop downward to the nest,
  And day drops downward to the sea,
And song and wing are fain to rest,
  The lark's dear wisdom guideth me,
And I too turn within my door,
Content to dream, and sing no more.

'Madeleine Bridges'
(Mary Ainge de Vere)

Shelley's skylark
(The Neighbourhood of Leghorn: March 1887)

Somewhere afield here something lies
In Earth's oblivious eyeless trust
That moved a poet to prophecies –
A pinch of unseen, unguarded dust:

The dust of the lark that Shelley heard,
And made immortal through times to be –
Though it only lived like another bird,
And knew not its immortality:

Lived its meek life; then, one day, fell –
A little ball of feather and bone;
And how it perished, when piped farewell,
And where it wastes, are alike unknown.

Maybe it rests in the loam I view,
Maybe it throbs in a myrtle's green,
Maybe it sleeps in the coming hue
Of a grape on the slopes of yon inland scene.

Go find it, faeries, go and find
That tiny pinch of priceless dust,
And bring a casket silver-lined,
And framed of gold that gems encrust;

And we will lay it safe therein,
And consecrate it to endless time;
For it inspired a bard to win
Ecstatic heights in thought and rhyme.

Thomas Hardy
(1840–1928)

On a forsaken lark's nest

Lo, where left 'mid the sheaves, cut down by the iron-
    fanged reaper,
Eating its way as it clangs fast through the wavering wheat,
Lies the nest of a lark, whose little brown eggs could not keep her
As she, affrighted and scared, fled from the harvester's feet.

Ah, what a heartful of song that now will never awaken,
Closely packed in the shell, awaited love's fostering,
That should have quickened to life what, now a-cold and forsaken,
Never, enamoured of light, will meet the dawn on the wing.

Ah, what pæans of joy, what raptures no mortal can measure,
Sweet as honey that's sealed in the cells of the honeycomb,
Would have ascended on high in jets of mellifluous pleasure,
Would have dropped from the clouds to nest in its
    gold-curtained home.

Poor, pathetic brown eggs! Oh, pulses that never will quicken
Music mute in the shell that hath been turned to a tomb!
Many a sweet human singer, chilled and adversity-stricken,
Withers benumbed in a world his joy might have helped to illume.

Mathilde Blind
(1841–1896)

The song in the dell

I know a way
Of hearing what the larks and linnets say:
    The larks tell of the sunshine and the sky;
    The linnets from the hedges make reply,
And boast of hidden nests with mocking lay.

I know a way
Of keeping near the rabbits at their play:
    They tell me of the cool and shady nooks
    Where waterfalls disturb the placid brooks
That I may go and frolic in the spray.

I know a way
Of catching dewdrops on a night in May,
And threading them upon a spear of green,
That through their sides translucent may be seen
The sparkling hue that emeralds display.

I know a way
Of trapping sunbeams as they nimbly play
At hide-and-seek with meadow-grass and flowers,
And holding them in store for dreary hours
When winds are chill and all the sky is gray.

I know a way
Of stealing fragrance from the new-mown hay
And storing it in flasks of petals made,
To scent the air when all the flowers fade
And leave the woodland world to sad decay.

I know a way
Of coaxing snowflakes in their flight to stay
So still awhile, that, as they hang in air,
I weave them into frosty lace, to wear
About my head upon a sultry day.

Charles Edward Carryl
(1841–1920)

Lark-eating...

Lark-eating, which revolts us even more than wheat-ear eating, is, alas! too common and wide-spread in the country to be suppressed... It will not soon be ended – there are too many Britons with the Italian's debased passion for a song-bird's flesh. But the feeling of intense disgust and even abhorrence the practice arouses in all lovers of nature grows, and will continue to grow; and we may look forward to the time when the feeders on skylarks of to-day will be dead and themselves eaten by worms, and will have no successors in all these islands.

William Henry Hudson
(1841–1922)

Lark in the upper air

Like a lark to glide aloof
Under the cloud-festooned roof,
That with a turning of the wings
Light and darkness from him flings;
To drift in air, the circled earth
Spreading still its sunned girth;
To hear the sheep-bells dimly die
Till the lifted clouds were nigh,
In breezy belts of upper air
Melting into aether rare;
And when the silent height were won,
And all in lone air stood the sun,
To sing scarce heard, and singing fill
The airy empire at his will;
To hear his strain descend less loud

On to ledges of grey cloud;
And fainter, finer, trickle far
To where the listening uplands are;
To pause – then from his gurgling bill
Let the warbled sweetness rill,
And down the welkin, gushing free,
Hark the molten melody;
In fits of music till sunset
Starting the silver rivulet;
Sweetly then and of free act
To quench the fine-drawn cataract;
And in the dews beside his nest
To cool his plumy throbbing brest.

Gerard Manley Hopkins
(1844–1889)

The sea and the skylark

On ear and ear two noises too old to end
  Trench – right, the tide that ramps against the shore;
  With a flood or a fall, low lull-off or all roar,
Frequenting there while moon shall wear and wend.

Left hand, off land, I hear the lark ascend,
  His rash-fresh re-winded new-skeined score
  In crisps of curl off wild winch whirl, and pour
And pelt music, till none's to spill or spend.

How these two shame this shallow and frail town!
  How ring right out our sordid turbid time,
Being pure! We, life's pride and cared-for crown,

Have lost that cheer and charm of earth's past prime:
  Our make and making break, are breaking, down
To man's last dust, drain fast towards man's first slime.

The caged skylark

As a dare-gale skylark scanted in a dull cage
  Man's mounting spirit in his bone-house, mean house,
        dwells –
  That bird beyond the remembering his free fells;
This is drudgery, day-labouring-out life's age.

Though aloft on turf or perch or poor low stage,
  Both sing sometimes the sweetest, sweetest spells,
  Yet both droop deadly sometimes in their cells
Or wring their barriers in bursts of fear or rage.

Not that the sweet-fowl, song-owl, needs no rest –
Why, hear him, hear him babble and drop down to his nest,
  But his own nest, wild nest, no prison.

Man's spirit will be flesh-bound when found at best,
But uncumbered: meadow-down is not distressed
  For a rainbow footing it nor he for his bones risen.

Gerard Manley Hopkins

Riding adown the country lanes

Riding adown the country lanes
  One day in spring,
Heavy at heart with all the pains
  Of man's imagining: –

The mist was not yet melted quite
  Into the sky:
The small round sun was dazzling white,
  The merry larks sang high:

The grassy northern slopes were laid
  In sparkling dew,
Out of the slow-retreating shade
  Turning from sleep anew:

Deep in the sunny vale a burn
  Ran with the lane,
O'erhung with ivy, moss and fern
  It laughed in joyful strain:

And primroses shot long and lush
  Their cluster'd cream:
Robin and wren and amorous thrush
  Carol'd above the stream:

The stillness of the lenten air
  Call'd into sound
The motions of all life that were
  In field and farm around:

So fair it was, so sweet and bright,
    The jocund Spring
Awoke in me the old delight
    Of man's imagining,

Riding adown the country lanes:
    The larks sang high. –
O heart! for all thy griefs and pains
    Thou shalt be loth to die.

Robert Bridges
(1844–1930)

Larks

What voice of gladness, hark!
    In heaven is ringing?
From the sad fields the lark
    Is upward winging.

High through the mournful mist that blots our day
Their songs betray them soaring in the grey.
        See them! Nay, they
In sunlight swim; above the furthest stain
Of cloud attain; their hearts in music rain
        Upon the plain.

Sweet birds, far out of sight
    Your songs of pleasure
Dome us with joy as bright
    As heaven's best azure.

Robert Bridges

The lark

He rose, and singing passed from sight –
A shadow kindling with the sun,
His joy ecstatic flamed, till light
And heavenly song were one.

John Bannister Tabb
(1845–1909)

Evolution

Out of the dusk a shadow,
  Then, a spark;
Out of the cloud a silence,
  Then, a lark;
Out of the heart a rapture,
  Then, a pain;
Out of the dead cold ashes,
  Life again.

John Bannister Tabb

The Ancoats skylark

...Perhaps it was difficult for people to understand the extraordinary ignorance of town children in such districts as he was referring to, respecting the commonest natural objects. The other day he was inspecting a school in Ancoats, and the boys in the first class were repeating some poetry they had learnt about a skylark. He enquired whether anyone had ever seen a lark; there was a silence, but a boy presently held out his hand to signify he wished to speak, and on his saying,

'Well, where did you see a lark?' he answered, 'In the public-house at the corner of the street, in a cage.' He (Mr Oakeley) thought, 'Poor caged lark, and poor caged little lad.' - *Speech of Mr H.E. Oakeley, H.M. Senior Inspector of Schools, at the opening of the Manchester School Board Central Higher Grade School, July, 1884.*

The day was hot, the summer sun
   Pierced through the city gloom;
It touched the teacher's anxious face,
   It brightened all the room.

Around him children of the poor,
   Ill fed, with clothing scant,
The flotsam of the social wreck,
   The heirs of work and want.

The sunlight glorified their rags
   As he essayed to tell
The wonders of the country side,
   Of clough, and burn, and fell.

For, as he spoke, the schoolroom walls
   Kept fading from his sight,
He stood upon his native hills,
   All bathed in golden light.

Once more he heard the skylark sing,
   Sing right at heaven's door,
And fill the span of earth beneath
   With music from its store.

A summer cloud sailed o'er the sky,
  The sunlight passed away,
The teacher saw his puny boys
  With city grime all grey.

'And which of you has heard a lark,
  'Or seen its fluttering wings,
'As o'er the hills of Lancashire
  'It rises and it sings?'

'Ah, no, the hills are far away,
  'From Ancoats' toil and stress.
'The skylark, have you heard its song
  'Or seen its homely dress?'

A silence fell upon the class,
  On all the listening ring,
Then one said, 'Sir, I've seen a lark,
  'And heard him loudly sing.'

'And where, my little Ancoats lad,
  'Did you the lavrock see?'
''Twas in a wooden cage that hung
  'Outside the "Cotton Tree".'

Alas, poor bird! chained thus amidst
  The city's smoke and gloom,
No more for thee the sunny sky,
  The wild flower's sweet perfume.

Alas, poor caged Ancoats boy!
  That freedom's song ne'er heard
Trilled o'er the fells of Lancashire
  By this bright poet-bird.

Alas the teacher, who of hills
　　The dear delight is known,
And, now amidst the city slums,
　　Is bound by walls of stone.

And yet the teacher finds it joy
　　To help the laddish throng;
The boy is blithe, and strong of heart,
　　The bird ne'er fails in song.

So may the teacher's magic art,
　　The bird's melodious ditty,
The sunshine of the boyish heart,
Ne'er fade from out the city.

Until the time once more shall come,
　　When free from bars and ties,
The bonny lavrock's song shall thrill
　　Through all the Ancoats skies.

William E.A. Axon
(1846–1910)

Out of tune

'Spirits are not finely touched
But to fine issues.'

In a certain manufacturing town, of no great size, there lived a musician. For the most part he gained his living by playing at concerts and giving lessons; but he was young, ardent, and clever, and he had always nursed a hope that he might one day be a great composer. He felt a soul of music within him, that wanted to come out and express itself. But, though he had had a complete training in composition, and had written much music and published a little, no one took any notice of what he composed; it was too good to sell well (so he used to say and perhaps it was true), and he had never had a chance of having any of his larger works performed in public. And he began to get rather irritable and impatient, so that his wife was sometimes at her wits' end to know how to cheer him up and set him to work once more with a good heart.

Great was the poor man's delight when one day a letter arrived from the town clerk, to tell him that on the approaching visit of the Prince of Wales to open the new Town Hall, a grand concert was to be given, in which works by natives of the town were to be performed; and that he was invited to write a short cantata for voices and orchestra. A liberal sum was to be paid to him, and he was to train his own choir, to have the best artists from London to help him, and to conduct his composition himself. The news put him in such a state of high spirits that now the prudent wife was obliged to pour a little cold water on his ambition, and tell him that he must not expect too much success all at once. But she made him comfortable in their little parlour, and kept the neighbours from breaking in upon his work; and for some time the cantata went on at a flowing pace, until nearly half of it was done.

After a while, however, the musician's brain began to rebel against being kept in all day hard at work, and to refuse to keep quiet and rest in soothing sleep at night. It said as plainly as possible – 'If you will go on driving me in harness all day long, I shall be obliged to fidget at night, and what is more, it is quite impossible for me to do such good work in the day as I used to. So take your choice: either you must give me repose sometimes, or I must cease to be able to find you beautiful melodies, and to show you how to treat them to the best advantage.' But the musician did not know that his brain was complaining in this way, though his wife heard it quite well; and he

111

went on driving it harder than ever, whipping it up and spurring it on, though it had hardly any strength left to pull the cantata along with it. And all this time he was shutting himself away from his friends, who used formerly to come often and refresh him with a friendly chat in the evenings; he refused to go with his wife and visit the very poor people whom they had been in the habit of comforting out of their slender store; he lost his temper several times with his pupils, and one day boxed a boy's ears for playing a wrong note twice over, so that the father threatened to summon him before the magistrates and have him fined for assault; and his wife began at last to fear that his stroke of good luck had done him more harm than good.

One morning he got up after a restless night, in which his poor brain had been complaining as usual without being taken any notice of, and settled himself down in the parlour after breakfast with the cantata, feeling worried and tired both in his body and mind. With great labour and trouble he finished the last chorus of his first part, and uttered a sign of relief. The next thing to be done was to write the first piece of the second part, which was to be an air for a single voice, and was to be sung at the concert by one of the best singers in the country. All the rest of the cantata had been thought out carefully before he began to write; but this song, for which beautiful words were chosen from an old poet, had never worked itself out in his brain so as to satisfy him. And now the poor brain was called upon for inspiration, just at a time when it was hardly fit even to do a clerk's work.

He tried to spur it up with a pipe of tobacco, but not a bit would it budge. Then he took a dose of *sal volatile*; but the effect of it only lasted a few minutes, and then he felt even more stupid than before. Then he opened the window and looked out into their little back-garden, just as a gleam of sunshine shot down through a murky sky. This made him feel a little better, and he returned to his desk and sat for a few moments looking at the words which he was to set to music, feeling almost as if he were going to make a little way. But

112

the sunshine had also made the canary in the window feel a little warm-hearted, and it burst out into such a career of song, that the room seemed to be echoing all over with its strains. And all his own music fled at once out of the distracted composer's head.

'You little noisy fiend!' he cried angrily, 'putting in your miserable little twopenny pipe, when a poor human artist is struggling to sing. Don't you know, you little wretch, that art is long and time is fleeting?'

He jumped up, took down the cage with an ungentle hand, and carried it into another room, where he drew a heavy shawl over it and shut the door. The canary's song was stifled, but the musician's song was not a bit the better for it. And after a while there came another annoyance. The house was small and not very solidly built, and though the room where he was at work did not look out on the street, any street-calls, bands, hurdy-gurdys, or such like noise-making enemies, could be heard quite distinctly. This time it was a street-boy whistling a tune; it was not a bad tune, and it was whistled with a good heart; indeed the boy put so much energy into his performance, that he must have been in very high spirits. And why did he stop there so long? Generally they passed by, and the tails of their tunes disappeared in the distance, or they turned down the next street. But this one was clearly stopping there on purpose to annoy the composer.

He went softly into the front room, keeping out of sight from the window. He was seized with a desire to wreak vengeance on this tormentor, but he was not quite clear on how to do it, and must survey his ground first. Stepping behind the window-curtain, he peeped out between the curtain and the window-frame, and saw a small boy, whistling hard, with a long string in his hand, which descended into the area below. The musician stood on tiptoe, and looked down into the area; it was a sort of relief to him to see what this urchin was about. At the end of the string he perceived a dead mouse, which was being made to jump up and down and counterfeit

113

life, as well as was possible under the circumstances, for the benefit of a young cat of the household, who was lying in wait for it, springing on it, and each time finding it drawn away from her just as she thought her claws were fast fixed in it. This boy was in fact an original genius, who had invented this way of amusing himself; he called it cat-fishing, and it was excellent sport.

The musician suddenly flung up the window, and faced the boy, who seemed by no means disconcerted; he only left off whistling and looked hard at the musician.

'What are you doing with the cat?' said the latter, with all the dignity he could put on.

'What business have you to meddle with my cat, and make that infernal din in front of my house?'

The boy began slowly to haul up the string, looking all the while steadily at the composer.

'I say, guv'nor,' he said, with a mock show of friendly interest, 'do you know as you've got a blob of ink at the end o'your nose?'

The composer was taken aback. He certainly did not know it, but nothing was more likely, considering how he had been pulling his moustache and scratching his head with fingers which, as he glanced at them, showed some traces of ink.

He put his hand involuntarily to his nose, and half turned to the glass over the chimney-piece. There was not a stain there; the nose was innocent of ink. Instantly he returned to the window, but the boy was gone; all that was left of him was a distant sound of 'There's nae luck aboot the house' far down the street. The composer went gloomily back to his study, without a particle of music in his brain; the canary and the whistler had driven it all away. He sat down mechanically at his desk, but he might as well have sat down at the kitchen-table and tried to make it play like a piano.

He got up once more, and looked out of the window. The sun was again shining, and the little garden, fenced in between brick walls which caught the sunshine, and enlivened with a few annuals (for it was early summer), did not look altogether uninviting. At the end of it was a little arbour which he had built himself, and a rose tree that he had planted against it was already beginning to blossom. The composer thought he would go and quiet himself down in this little arbour, and try and get his thoughts fixed upon the air he was to write. Out he went, and seated there, began to feel more at ease. After a while he began to think once more of the old poet's lines; and feeling as if the music were coming into his brain again, went and fetched his manuscript and his pen and ink, to be ready in case he should have musical thoughts to write down.

Suddenly there broke in upon his peace the loud, shrill song of a wren. It was close to him, just outside the arbour; and when a wren sings close to you, it pierces your ear like the shrillest whistle ever blown by a schoolboy. It was unconscious of the presence of the composer so close to its nest, which it had built in the branches of the rose-tree that climbed up outside; and it hopped down for a moment on the gravel just in front of the arbour to pick up some fragment of food.

The composer's nerves were quite unstrung by its sudden outburst of self-asserting song; it was an insult to music, to the poet, and to himself. No sooner did the tiny bird appear, as complacent and hearty as all wrens are, than he seized the ink-bottle, and like Luther at Wittemburg, flung it wildly at the little fiend that thus dared to disturb his peace. Of course he missed his aim; of course he broke the ink- bottle and spilt the ink; and alas! when he returned from picking up the bits, a splash from the bottle had fallen in a grand slanting puddle over the neat manuscript of the last page of the chorus which concluded his second part. And as he stood beholding it in dismay, lo! the voice of that irrepressible little wren, as shrill and pert as ever, only a little further off!

If the musician had not quarrelled with his brain, and if the struggle between them had not put his nerves all out of tune – if he had been then the gentle and sweet-tempered artist he generally was

115

– he would have laughed at the idea of such a little pigmy flouting him in this ridiculous way. As it was, he growled under his breath that everything was against him, crushed his hat on his head, took the manuscript into the house and locked it up in a drawer, wrote a hurried note to his wife, who had gone out, to say he had gone for a long walk and would not be back till late, and sallied out of the house where no peace was any longer possible for him.

He walked fast, and was soon out of the town and among the lanes. They were decked with the full bloom of the wild roses, and the meadows were golden with buttercups; but these the composer did not even see. Birds sang everywhere, but he did not hear them. He was just conscious that the sun was shining on him, but his eyes were fixed on the ground, and his mind was so full of his own troubles that there was no room in it for anything nicer to enter there.

He was thinking that his song would never be written, for he could not bear to write anything that should be unworthy of those words, or second-rate as music; and it seemed as if his brain would never again yield him any music that he could be satisfied with. 'I shall be behindhand,' he thought to himself. 'I shall have to write and say I can't carry out my undertaking; my one chance will be lost and all my hopes with it. I shall lose my reputation and my pupils, and then there will be nothing left but beggary and a blighted life!'. And he worked himself up into such a dreadful state that when he was crossing a river by a bridge, it did actually occur to him whether it would not be as well to jump over the parapet and put an end to his troubles once and for all. His mind was so full of himself that for a moment he forgot even his wife and child, and all his friends and well-wishers.

He stood by the parapet for some minutes looking over. The swallows and sand-martins were gliding up and down, backwards and forwards through the bridge, catching their food and talking to themselves. A big trout rose to secure a mayfly from the deep pool below, and sent a circle of wavelets spreading far and wide. A kingfisher flashed under the bridge, all blue and green, and shot away

116

noiselessly up the stream; and then a red cow or two came down to drink, and after drinking stood in the water up to their knees, and looked sublimely cool and comfortable. And the river itself flowed on with a gentle rippling talk in the sunshine, hushing as it entered the deep pool, and passing under the bridge slowly and almost silently – 'like an *andante* passing into an *adagio,*' said the musician to himself; and he walked on with eyes no longer fixed on the ground, for even this little glimpse of beauty from the bridge had been medicine to the brain, and it wanted more – it wanted to see and to hear more things that were beautiful and healing.

He went on, still gloomy, but his gloom was no longer an angry and sullen one. Through his eyes and ears came sensations that gradually gladdened his heart, and relieved the oppression on his brain: he began to notice the bloom on the hedges and in the fields; and the singing of the larks high in the air, though he hardly attended to it, made part of the joyousness of nature which was beginning to steal into his weary being. Presently he came to a little hamlet, hardly more than a cottage or two, but with a little church standing at right angles to the road. The churchyard looked inviting, for rose-bushes were blooming among the graves, and it was shut out from the road by a high wall, so that he would be unobserved there. He walked in and sat down on a tombstone to rest.

He had not been there long, and was beginning to feel calmed and quieted, when there broke out on him from the ivied wall the very same shrill wren's song that had so wounded his feelings in the morning. It sent a momentary pang through him. There started up before his eyes the broken ink-bottle, the smeared page, the bitter vexation and worry, and the song not even yet begun. But the battle of body and brain was no longer being waged, and as the tiny brown bird sang again and again, and always the same strain, he began to wonder how such cheerful music could ever have so maddened him. It brought to his mind a brilliant bit of Scarlatti, in which a certain lively passage comes up and up again, always the same, like a clear, strong spring of water bubbling up with unflagging energy, and with a never-failing supply of joyousness. And the wren and Scarlatti getting the better of him, he passed out of the churchyard, and actually began to feel that he was hungry.

Just across the road was a thatched cottage, standing in a little garden gay with early summer flowers; beehives stood on each side of the entrance, and a vine hung on the wall. It looked inviting, and the musician stepped over the little stile, and tapped at the door, which was open. A woman of middle age came forward.

'Can you tell me,' said he, 'Whether there is an inn anywhere near where I could get some bread and cheese?'

She answered that there was no inn nearer than the next village, two miles away. 'But you look tired and pale, sir. Come in and have a morsel before you go on; and a cup of tea will be like to do you good. Sit you down in the porch and rest a bit, and I'll bring you something in a moment.'

The musician thanked her, and sat down in the porch by the beehives. It was delicious there! – bees, flowers, sunshine; on the ground the shadows of the vine-leaves that were clustering unkempt above his head; in the distance golden meadows and elm-trees, and the faint blue smoke of the town he had left behind him. Outside the porch hung a cage, in which was a skylark, the favourite cage-bird of the poor; it had been interrupted in its song by the stranger's arrival, but now began again, and sang with as good a heart and as lusty a voice as its free brethren in the blue of heaven.

'What a stream of song!' thought the musician. 'He sings like good old Haydn! We can't do that now. We don't pour out our hearts in melody, and do just what we like with our tunes.'

The lark ceased for a moment, and the ticking of the big clock within the cottage suddenly called up in his mind the *Andante* of the *Clock Symphony*, and the two bassons ticking away in thirds with that peculiar comical solemnity of theirs; and he leant back in the porch and laughed inside to himself till the lark began to sing again.

118

Then he went on mentally to the last *Allegro Vivace,* and caught up by its extraordinary force and vivacity, his brain was dancing away in a flood of delicious music, when the woman came out to him with a cup of tea and bread and butter.

'How that bird does sing!' he said to her. 'It has done me worlds of good already!'

'Ah,' she answered, 'he has been a good friend to us too. It was my boy that gave him to me – him as is away at sea. He sings pretty nigh all the year round, and sometimes he do make a lot of noise; but we never gets tired of him, he minds us so of our lad. Ah, 'tis a bad job when your only boy will go for to be a sailor. I never crosses the road to church of a stormy morning and sees the ripples on the puddles, but I thinks of the stormy ocean and my poor son!'

The musician asked more about the sailor; and he was shown his likeness, and various relics of him that the fond mother had cherished up. And when he rose to go he shook hands with the woman warmly, and told her that he would one day bring his wife and ask for another cup of tea. Then he started off once more, refreshed as much by the milk of human kindness as by the tea and bread and butter.

He soon began to feel sleepy, and looked for a quiet spot where he could lie down in the shade. Crossing two or three fields he came to a little dingle, where a stream flowed by a woodside; on the other side was a meadow studded with elms and beeches, and under the shade of one of these, close to the brook, and facing the wood, he lay down, and was soon fast asleep.

He was woken up by a musical note so piercing, yet so exquisitely sweet, a *crescendo* note of such wonderful power and volume, that he started up on his elbow and looked all round him. It was not repeated; but in a minute or two there came from the wood opposite him a liquid trill; then an inward murmur; then a loud jug-jug-jug; and then the nightingale began to sing in earnest, and carried the musician with him into a kind of paradise. He did not think now of the great

119

composer; this was not Beethoven or Mozart; this was something new, and altogether rich and strange.

Every time the bird ceased he was in suspense as to what would come next; and what came next was as surprising as what went before. At last the nightingale ceased, and dropped into the thick underwood; but the musician lay there still, and mused and dozed.

At length he started up and looked at his watch; it was past seven o'clock. He hurried off homewards in the cool air, refreshed and quieted, thinking of nothing but the things around him, and now and then of the cottage, the lark, the brookside, and the nightingale. But presently there came into his recollection the old poet's lines, and he repeated them over to himself, for they seemed in harmony with his mood, and with the coolness, and the sunset. Then as a star comes out in the twilight, there came upon his mind a strain worthy to be married to immortal verse; like the star, it grew in brightness every moment, until he could see it clear and full. In a moment paper and pencil were in his hand, and the thought was fixed beyond all fear of forgetting. By the time he reached home, the whole strain was worked out in his mind, and he wrote the first draft of it that same evening, as he sat contented in his parlour, with his wife sewing by his side.

After this nothing went wrong with the cantata. It was finished, it was a great success, and the music to the old poet's words was enthusiastically encored. The audience called loudly for the composer, and the Prince of Wales sent for him, and congratulated him warmly. And the day after the concert he took his wife out into the country, and they had tea at the cottage; the lark sang to them, the flowers were alive with murmuring bees, and the eventful day, not even keeping from her the thought that had passed through his mind on the bridge.

When he had finished, she laid her hand on his, and said, in her comfortable, womanly way –

photograph by Chris Knights

'You were out of tune, dear, that's what it was. And you can't make beautiful music, if you're out of tune: everything you see and hear jars on you. You must tell me next time you feel yourself getting out of tune, and we'll come out here and set you all right again.'

They went comfortably back to the town, after a day of complete happiness. As they neared their own door, they saw the street-boy leaning again over their railings, and cat-fishing as usual in the area. He was whistling with all his might; but this time it was 'Weel may the keel row'. They took it as a good omen; and the astonished urchin found himself pounced on from behind, carried into the house by main force, and treated with cake, and all manner of good things, while the musician sat down to the piano and played him all the beautiful tunes he could remember. He did not come to fish in their area any more after this; but a few days later he was heard whistling 'Vedrai Carino' with an abstracted air, as he leant over a neighbour's railings, amusing himself with his favourite pastime.

W. Warde Fowler
(1847–1921)

The sky lark as a wind-compass, and a continuous songster

If at any time when you are out in the country and you wish to know from which direction the wind is blowing, look up at the nearest skylark soaring in the air, notice in which direction its head is facing, and there you are! 'Why,' asks the reader, 'should this be, and how comes it soars and sings with its head towards the breeze, thus acting as a feathered wind-compass!

Wherever Larks abound, let it be a calm day or blowing a regular hurricane, providing it is between the months of January and July, some birds are almost sure to be on the wing, singing such

121

captivating music that we can well understand and appreciate the exquisite Ode which Shelley wrote to this 'scorner of the ground', as also the many further beautiful poems which have been written by George Meredith, Eric Mackay, and other poets.

Even in the country I meet some people who find difficulty in forecasting the direction of the wind. If they had Skylarks in their neighbourhood, and would only take notice of the birds up aloft, their difficulty might at once be overcome.

It must not be supposed, however, from the foregoing, that the Larks' period of song is restricted to the first seven months of the year. That is its most continuous songtime, but after the moulting season – August to Mid-September – it resumes its sweet strains and sings on until November or December, although not with such continuity as during the first six or seven months of the year.

There is very often a warm interval in February, sometimes a few days earlier and sometimes later, but as a rule it happens that a week or so of mild sunny weather occurs about this time. Released from the grip of the frost, the streams trickle forth from the fields and pour into the ditches, so that while walking along the footpath there is a murmur all around coming from the rush of water. The murmur of the poets is indeed louder in February than in the more pleasant days of summer, for then the growth of aquatic grasses checks the flow and stills it, whilst in February, every stone, or flint, or lump of chalk divides the current and causes a vibration. With this murmur of water, and mild time, the rooks caw incessantly, and the birds at large essay to utter their welcome of the sun. The wet furrows reflect the rays so that the dark earth gleams, and in the slight mist that stays farther away the light pauses and fills the vapour with radiance. Through this luminous mist the larks race after each other twittering, and as they turn aside, swerving in their swift flight, their white breasts appear for a moment. As while standing by a pool the fishes come into sight, emerging as they swim round from the shadow of the deeper water, so the larks dart over the low hedge, and through the mist, and pass before you, and are gone again. All at once one checks his pursuit, forgets the immediate object, and rises, singing as he soars. The notes fall from the air over the dark wet earth, over the dank grass, and broken withered fern of the hedges, and listening to them it seems for a moment spring. There is sunshine in the song: the lark and the light are one. He gives us a few minutes of summer in February days. In May he rises before as yet the dawn is come, and the sunrise flows down to us under through his notes. On his breast, high above the earth, the first rays fall as the rim of the sun edges up at the eastward hill. The lark and the light are as one, and wherever he glides over the wet furrows the glint of the sun goes with him. Anon, alighting, he runs between the lines of the green corn. In hot summer, when the open hillside is burned with bright light, the larks are then singing and soaring. Stepping up the hill laboriously, suddenly a lark starts into the light and pour forth a rain of unwearied notes overhead, With bright light, and sunshine, and sunrise, and blue skies the bird is so associated in the mind, that even to see him in the frosty days of winter, at least assures us that summer will certainly return.

Richard Jefferies
(1848–1887)

The lark

...The hawk...seems to descend nearly in a perpendicular line.

The lark does the same, and often from a still greater height, descending so swift that by comparison with other birds it looks as if she must be dashed to pieces; but within a few yards of the ground the wings are outstretched, and she glides along some distance before alighting. This latter motion makes it difficult to tell where a lark actually does alight. So, too, with snipe: they appear to drop in a

123

corner of the brook, and you feel positive that a certain bunch of rushes is the precise place; but before you get there the snipe is up again under your feet, ten or fifteen yards closer than you supposed, having shot along hidden by the banks, just above the water, out of sight.

Marshall Cavendish
Picture Library

Sometimes, after soaring to an unusual elevation, the lark comes down, as it were, in one or two stages: after dropping say fifty feet the wings are employed, and she shoots forward horizontally some way, which checks the velocity. Repeating this twice or more, she reaches the ground safely. In rising up to sing she often traces a sweeping spiral in the air at first, going round once or twice; after which, seeming to settle on the line she means to ascend, she goes up almost perpendicularly in a series of leaps, as it were – pausing a moment to gather impetus, and then shooting upwards till a mere speck in the sky. When ten or twelve larks are singing at once, all within a narrow radius – a thing that may be often witnessed from these downs in the spring – the charm of their vivacious notes is greater than when one solitary bird alone discourses sweet music which is lost in the blue dome overhead.

At that time they seem to feed only a few minutes consecutively, and then, as if seized with an uncontrollable impulse, rush up into the air to deliver a brief song, descend, and repeat the process for hours. They have a way, too, of rising but six or eight yards above the earth, spreading the wings out and keeping them nearly still, floating slowly forward all the while uttering one sweet note softly. The sward by the roadside appears to have a special attraction for them; they constantly come over from the arable fields, alight there, and presently return. In the early spring, when love-making is in full progress, the cornfields where the young green blades are just showing become the scene of the most amusing rivalry. Far as the eye can see across the ground it seems alive with larks – chasing each other to and fro, round and round, with excited calls, flying close to the surface, continually alighting, and springing up again. A gleam of sunshine and a warm south wind bring forth these merry antics. So like in general hue is the lark to the lumps of brown earth that even at a few paces it is difficult to distinguish her. Some seem always to remain in the meadows; but the majority frequent the arable land, and especially the cornfields on the slopes of the downs, where they may be found in such numbers as rival or perhaps exceed those of any other bird.

At first sight starlings seem more numerous; but this arises from their habit of gathering together in such vast flocks, blackening the earth where they alight. But you may walk a whole day across the downs and still find larks everywhere; so that though scattered abroad they probably equal or exceed the starlings, who show so much more. They are by no means timid, being but little disturbed here: you can get near enough to watch every motion, and if they rise it is only to sing. They never seem to know precisely where they are going to alight – as if, indeed, they were nervously particular and must find a clod that pleases them, picking and choosing with the greatest nicety.

Richard Jefferies

Margaritae sorori
I. M.

A late lark twitters from the quiet skies,
And from the west,
Where the sun, his day's work ended,
Lingers as in content,
There falls on the old, gray city
An influence luminous and serene,
A shining peace.

The smoke ascends
In a rosy-and-golden haze. The spires
Shine and are changed. In the valley
Shadows rise. The lark sings on. The sun
Closing his benediction,
Sinks, and the darkening air
Thrills with a sense of the triumphing night –
Night with her train of stars
And her great gift of sleep.

So be my passing!
My task accomplish'd and the long day done,
My wages taken, and in my heart
Some late lark singing,
Let me be gather'd to the quiet west,
The sundown splendid and serene,
Death.

William Ernest Henley
(1849–1903)

To a lark

O little singing bird,
   If I could word
In as sweet human phrase
   Thy hymn of praise:

The world should hearken me
   As I do thee,
And I should heed no more
   Than thou, but soar.

Francis William Bourdillon
(1852–1921)

The veery

The moon beams over Arno's vale in silver flood were pouring,
When I first heard the nightingale a long-lost love deploring.
So passionate, so full of pain, it sounded strange and eerie;
I longed to hear a simpler strain, – the wood-notes of the veery.

127

The laverock sings a bonny lay above the Scottish heather;
It sprinkles down from far away like light and love together;
He drops the golden notes to greet his brooding mate, his dearie;
I only know one song more sweet, – the vespers of the veery.

In English gardens, green and bright and full of fruity treasure,
I heard the blackbird with delight repeat his merry measure:
The ballad was a pleasant one, the tune was loud and cheery,
And yet, with every setting sun. I listened for the veery.

But far away, and far away, the tawny thrush is singing;
New England woods, at close of day, with that clear chant are
    ringing;
And when my light of life is low, and heart and flesh are weary,
I fain would hear, before I go, the wood-notes of the veery.

Henry Van Dyke
(1852–1933)

The skylark

Out of that palpitating speck of joy
There wells a sea of song beyond compare
Upon the morning and the evening air:
It swells like aspirations naught can cloy,
That naught in earth or heaven can e'er destroy;
Such rivulets of rhapsody declare
The bliss of singing through the clouds of care.
Is he the angel that Love doth employ
To melt the mist that veils the Spirit home,
Whose vital breath is music sweeter far
Than any motion of a soul or star?

That burns in blue, or brings to thought its bloom,
A marvel, and a miracle, exceeding rare:
The brightest concept in Creation's loom.

Thomas Burns
(1853–1938)

The country town

Every town has its own character, invariably English, but always distinctive. Stretched out, as a rule, along some main road, but thickening round the market-place, for generations its interests were parochial, local. Its prosperity hung on the seasons; foreign wars concerned it less than the disputes at the vestry, or than the election, or the fair; the corn crop, or the hops or fruit, mattered to it more than the price of Consols; and somehow, while the restricted but sufficient and simple life of the inhabitants impressed itself unconsciously upon the streets, the townsman as he traversed them breathed its influence unawares, and to this day one feels it. The customary High Street, glistening with reflected sunshine, has a charm beyond that which it derives constantly from the surrounding hills and valleys, and not dependent upon the fresh amplitude of air that enwraps the town so lovingly.

That the nearness of the open country contributes its effect of course is true. Very pleasant it is, as you walk about the old town, to glance through a gap between the houses – down some alley or backway, or under the entrance to an inn-yard – and catch a glimpse of green hillside a mile away under a great vista of sky telling of far horizons. You look up: as likely as not a rook is sailing overhead. You listen; and if the street chances to be quiet you may hear a lark singing. From a street in my own native town I have watched a hawk poised high in air; one spring day I heard, and looking up caught sight of, a passing cuckoo. Many birds are near at hand. Thrushes and blackbirds are melodious in the back gardens, swallows build under the eaves, now and again a wagtail comes down into the roadway. The summer evenings are vocal with the screaming of swifts; in the summer mornings, if you are up early enough, you may see rooks coolly walking in the streets as though they owned them. Pleasant odours come too. There are hours in June when the town is fragrant with the scent of new hay, though you do not see the meadows where it is making. The passing manure-waggon is at worst only half disagreeable, because, after all, it makes you think of farms, and another day the same waggon may bring in for atonement the scent of hops, or of the newly-opened heap of mangold... As you perceive, the shops and dwelling-houses are but a thin screen, a flimsy and often beautiful scene-painting, hiding the open country but not really shutting it out. Rather they frame the sky, and set the imagination dreaming of the fields over which it broods; and while they shut out the eyesores – the neglected farm, the squalid village, or the obtrusively new Cockney villas that too often disfigure the actual country – on the other hand they invite thoughts of the real beauty that lies beyond them. From out there behind the houses and across the valleys comes fancy of coppices full of primroses, hangers fringed with catkins, woodland hollows still open to the April sky, but soon to be curtained in with young leaves. There were never lovelier hedgerows, deeper meadows, more ample downs, or farms more peaceful, than those one is tempted to imagine from the High Street of a country town.

But delicious though all this may be, the street means more than this, and deserves to be looked upon affectionately for its own sake as a feature of the former English country-side. For the old towns – Salisbury and Basingstoke, Lewes, Dunstable, and the hundreds of others whose very names are inspiring – were not in their origin places where rural life ceased; they were the places where it grew tense and vital, and they stand now as a sort of ancient monuments, more interesting than Stonehenge or Old Sarum, of a past dear to every lover of the country.

George Bourne
(1863–1927)

Larks

All day in exquisite air
The song clomb an invisible stair,
Flight on flight, story on story,
Into the dazzling glory.

There was no bird, only a singing,
Up in the glory, climbing and ringing,
Like a small golden cloud at even,
Trembling 'twixt earth and heaven.

I saw no staircase, winding, winding,
Up in the dazzle, sapphire and blinding,
Yet round by round, in exquisite air,
The song went up the stair.

Katharine Tynan
(1889–1931)

from The charm of birds

The song of the bird now to be described is probably more familiar and distinct to everybody than any other. The skylark owes its fame to the manner of his singing; it is part of a conspicuous joy-flight.

131

The bird sings both ascending and descending. I have not myself timed individual Larks, but I am told that two minutes is an unusually long time for one performance. The bird is as visible as the song is audible, and there is no possibility of mistaking the singer or confusing it with any other bird: it compels recognition and attention. It has inspired fine lines of poetry, and there can be hardly a poet who has avoided all reference to it. In youth I preferred Shelley's to Wordsworth's poem on 'The Skylark', but in later years Wordsworth's 'A privacy of glorious light is thine' got a firmer grip and was more satisfying than all the similes, beautiful as they are, in Shelley's poem.

Ruskin, in Modern Painters, draws a distinction between 'Fancy' and 'Imagination'; the latter he exalts as incomparably the higher quality. He gives Shakespeare's 'Daffodils that come before the swallow dares, and take the wind of March with beauty', as one instance of Imagination; as an instance of Fancy he gives Milton's 'Pansy freaked with jet'. There can be no question which of these two expressions stirs us and endears the flower most. So is it with me in comparing Wordsworth's and Shelley's poems on the skylark. Shelley delights with the beauty of his poem, Wordsworth stirs our feeling for the bird.

I came across a small volume of verse written by a young airman in the war. There was no evidence that he knew Wordsworth's poem of the Skylark, but one of the experiences that he described as most pleasing or glorious was the sensation of being high up alone in the sunlight. When Wordsworth wrote 'A privacy of glorious light is thine', his imagination had penetrated to what man would feel in the Skylark's place. Without giving the bird human attributes, he had linked its flight and song to human feeling. This is an achievement in poetry that 'fancy', however beautiful, cannot accomplish.

The skylark becomes an essential feature of country life. I was walking from one plantation to another with an old woodman: it was a fine April day: we were crossing grass fields and skylarks were singing: as bird after bird rose about us the old man said aloud, but to himself rather than to me, 'Them lav'rocks mounts and sings'. They were part of his life...

Edward Grey
(Lord Grey of Fallodon, 1st Viscount)
(1862–1933)

Song of the larks at dawn

(I)

Shepherds who pastures seek
    At dawn may see
From Falterona's peak
    Above Camaldoli
Gleam, beyond forests and wildernesses bleak,
    Both shores of Italy.
Fallen apart are the terrible clouds of the morning
    And men lift up their eyes.

(II)

Birds that have circled and wound
    Through the chasms below
Disappear into belts profound
    Of fleet cloud, hail and snow.

The stripling land they behold not, nor high sea-bound;
    Out of harsh ravines they know,
Out of night – the Earth's own shadow from orbèd
    morning –
    They fear, they fear to rise.

(III)

Heaven's troubled continents
    Are rifted, torn,
Thunders in their forest tents
    Still seethe and sullenly mourn
When aloft, from the gulfs and the sheer ascents,
    Is a music born.
Hark to that music, laggard mists of the morning,
    And men, lift up your eyes.

(IV)

For scarce can eye see light
    When the ear's aware
That virginals exquisite
    Are raining from the air –
With sun and pale moon mingling their delight –
    Adorations everywhere!
The grass hears not, nor the stony summits of morning,
    But men lift up their eyes.

(V)

Eddy of fiery dust –
    Halo of rays –
Thrilling up, up, as they must
    Die of the life they praise,
The larks, the larks! I that to earth entrust
    Only their sleeping-place.
From rugged wolds and rock-bound valleys of morning
    The larks like mist arise.

(VI)

Earth sends them up from hills,
    Her wishes small,
Her cloud of griefs, her wills
    To burst from her own thrall
And to burn away what chains the soul or chills
    In the God and fount of all.
Open your gates, O ye cities faint for morning,
    And men, lift up your eyes.

(VII)

Open, Night's blue Pantheon,
    Thy dark roof-ring
For that escaping pæan
    Of tremblers on the wing
At the unknown threshold of the empyrean
    In myriads soft to sing.
Give way before them, temple-veils of the morning,
    And men, lift up your eyes.

(VIII)

O throngs caught unaware
    Whose glee is finding
The sun your father – who dare
    On the dark gales up-winding
Spill out on burning air your gossamer
    Of songs heaven-blinding –
Who beat the bounds and the wild marches of morning
    And take as yours the skies!

(IX)

They ascend ere the red beam
    On heaven grows strong
Into that amazing stream
    Of Dawn; and float along
In the future, for the future is their dream
    Who roof the world with song.
Open your flowers, O ye mountains spread for morning,
    And men, lift up your eyes!

(X)

They hang above the wave
    And are the voice
Of that light for which we crave –
    They flee from poise to poise –
They have forgotten the forgetful grave –
    In garlands they rejoice –
They dance upon the golden surge of morning
    That breaks our brooding skies.

Hark! it grows less and less
  But nothing mars
That rapture beyond guess
  Beyond our senses' bars.
They drink the virgin Light, the measureless
  And in it fade, like stars.
They have gone past, the dew-like spirits of morning
  Beyond the uplifted eyes.

(XII)

Between two lamps suspended
  Of Life and Death,
Sun-marshalled and moon-tended
  Man's swift soul journeyeth
To be borne out of the life it hath transcended
  Still, still on a breath:
For a day we too are the winged sons of the morning –
  To-day we will arise.

Herbert Trench
(1865–1923)

The interpretation of bird music

Nevertheless, one has only to listen to the Sky-lark to realize that superb aesthetic expression is attainable in the earlier phase of song, although the music is of the simplest character. As we learn from his cousins, the pipits, his primeval song can hardly have been more than the advertisement or accompaniment of a little aerial dance – a string of monosyllabic and disyllabic vocables timed to the beating of his wings, and changing with the successive stages of his performance. But generation after generation of robuster wings, in the joy of achievement have led him to higher and higher flights, ever accompanied by artistic changes in the phrasing and vocalization of the song. At length he gained the expression of pure serenity. More music would ruin it with excess of art; less play of z's and j's would extinguish it...

Walter Garstang
(1868–1949)

Prelude: The two choirs.

Oberon stirred and rubbed his eyes:
'I feel the Spring,' he said;
'My merry elves, arise, arise,
And sweep the cobwebs from the skies,
Ere Phoebus show his head!

'And gentle Puck, before a spark
Gleams from his orb of fire,
Go, bid the faithful morning Lark
Ascend his watch-tower in the dark,
And rouse my sleeping choir!'

Quickly was swept a pathway grey,
Night's sable curtain drawn,
And ere the faintest peep of day,
Up was the Lark and high away,
Loud heralding the dawn:

Swee! Swee! Swee! Swee!
Zwee-o! Zwee-o! Zwee-o! Zwee-o!

138

Sis-is-Swee! Sis-is-Swee!
Joo! Joo! Joo! Joo!
Jee-o! Jee-o! Sissy-sejoo!
Jit, jit, jit, jit, jit! Dzoo!
Zee, wee, wee, wee! Sis-is-is-Swee!
Swee-o, Swee! Swee-o, Swee!
Swee, swee, swee, swee, swee, swee, swee! Swee!

Awake! Awake!
In copse and break!
Night's reign is done;
Soon will the sun
Repaint the skies.
Arise! Arise! Ye birds below!
Pale fringes grow
And surely creep
Above the deep;
His breath of fire
Mounts ever higher;
His rosy frills
Adorn the hills.
Bestir! Bestir!
Each chorister!
Now cleave his spears
The ghostly meres
The mist he shakes
Through clouds he breaks;
He glints! He gleams!
His glorious beams
In triumph surge;
The orient verge
Is all ablaze
With golden rays.

Now are ye stirred!
Sing, every bird!
The Night is done,
The day begun;
Let every voice
Rejoice, rejoice!

Walter Garstang

The song of the skylark

In copse and hedgerow bird music is silent, and 'peace is the keynote of the surroundings', for the persistent robin is almost the only singer, though one may catch the occasional call note of bullfinch, wren, or another bird. Rising from the open fields, the skylark may now be seen; he was soaring and singing his sweet carol on September 21st, the first time for many weeks. I had been on the *qui vive* for his first breaking into song, and hasten to acknowledge that my friend was correct when he told me 'the skylark never sings in August'.

William Coles Finch
(1864–1944)

The downs

Oh! the downs high to the cool sky;
And the feel of the sun-warmed moss;
And each cardoon, like a full moon,
Fairy-spun of the thistle floss;
And the beech grove, and a wood dove,
And the trail where the shepherds pass;
And the lark's song, and the wind song,
And the scent of the parching grass!

John Galsworthy
(1867–1933)

A lark's song

Sweet, Sweet!
I rise to greet
The sapphire sky
The air slips by
On either side
As up I ride
On mounting wing,
And sing and sing –
Then reach my bliss,
The sun's great kiss;
And poise a space,
To see his face,
Sweet, sweet,
In radiant grace,
Ah, sweet! ah, sweet!

Sweet, sweet!
Beneath my feet
My nestlings call:
And down I fall
Unerring, true,
Through heaven's blue;
And haste to fill
Each noisy bill.
My brooding breast
Stills their unrest.
Sweet, sweet
Their quick hearts beat,
Safe in the nest:
Ah, sweet, sweet, sweet!
Ah, sweet!

Sweet, sweet
The calling sky
That bids me fly
Up-up-on high.
The claiming earth
It holds my nest
And draws me down
To where Love's crown
Of priceless worth
Awaits my breast.
Sweet, sweet!
Ah, this is best
And this most meet,
Sweet, sweet! ah, sweet!

Michael Fairless
(1869–1901)

from **At the white gate**

...I remember when, taking a grace from my road, I helped to mow Farmer Marler's ten-acre field, rich in ripe upstanding grass. The mechanism of the ancient reaper had given way under the strain of the home meadows, and if this crop was to be saved it must be by hand. I have kept the record of those days of joyous labour under the June sky. Men were hard to get in our village; old Dodden, who was over seventy, volunteered his services – he had done yeoman work with the scythe in his youth – and two of the farm hands with their master completed our strength.

We took our places under a five o'clock morning sky, and the larks cried down to us as we stood knee-deep in the fragrant dew-steeped grass, each man with his gleaming scythe poised ready for its sweeping swing. Old Dodden led by right of age and ripe experience: bent like a sickle, brown and dry as a nut, his face a tracery of innumerable wrinkles, he has never ailed a day, and the cunning of his craft was still with him. At first we worked stiffly, unreadily, but soon the monotonous motion possessed us with its insistent rhythm, and the grass bowed to each sibilant swish and fell in sweet-smelling swathes at our feet. Now and then a startled rabbit scurried through the miniature forest to vanish with a white flick of tail in the tangled hedge; here and there a mother lark was discovered sitting motionless, immovable upon her little brood; but save for those infrequent incidents we paced steadily on with no speech save the cry of the hone on the steel and the swish of the falling swathes. The sun rose high in the heaven and burnt on bent neck and bare and aching, arms, the blood beat and drummed in my veins with unwanted posture and exercise; I worked as a man who sees and hears in a mist. Once as I paused to whet my scythe, my eye caught the line of the untroubled hills strong and still in the broad sunshine; then to work again in the labouring, fertile valley...

...The grey dawn awoke and stole with trailing robes across earth's floor. At her footsteps the birds roused from sleep and cried a greeting; the sky flushed and paled conscious of coming splendour; and overhead a file of swans passed with broad strong flight to the reeded waters of the sequestered pool.

Another hour of silence while the light throbbed and flamed in the east; then the larks rose harmonious from a neighbouring field, the rabbits scurried with ears alert to their morning meal, the day had begun...

Michael Fairless

Kindness

Of the beauty of kindness I speak,
   Of a smile, of a charm
On the face it is pleasure to meet,
   That gives no alarm!

Of the soul that absorbeth itself
   In discovering good,
Of that power which outlasts health,
   As the spell of a wood.

Outlasts the sad fall of the leaves,
   And in winter is fine,
And from snow and from frost receives
   A garment divine.

Oh! well may the lark sing of this,
  As through rents of huge cloud
It breaks on blue gulfs that are bliss,
  For they make its heart proud

With the power of wings deployed
  In delightfullest air,
Yea, thus among things enjoyed
  Is kindness rare.

For even the weak with surprise
  Spread wings, utter song,
They can launch – in this blue they can rise,
  In this kindness are strong, –

They can launch like a ship into calm,
  Which was penn'd up by storm,
Which sails for the islands of balm
  Luxuriant and warm.

T. Sturge Moore
(1870–1940)

Cowslips and larks

I hear it said yon land is poor,
In spite of those rich cowslips there –
And all the singing larks it shoots
To heaven from the cowslips' roots.
But I, with eyes that beauty find,
And music ever in my mind,

145

Feed my thoughts well upon that grass
Which starves the horse, the ox, and ass.
So here I stand, two miles to come
To Shapwick and my ten-days-home,
Taking my summer's joy, although
The distant clouds are dark and low,
And comes a storm that, fierce and strong,
Has brought the Mendip Hills along:
Those hills that, when the light is there,
Are many a sunny mile from here.

W H Davies
(1871–1940)

A bird's anger

A summer's morning that has but one voice;
Five hundred stooks, like golden lovers, lean
Their heads together, in their quiet way,
And but one bird sings, of a number seen.

It is the lark, that louder, louder sings,
As though but this one thought possessed his mind:
'You silent robin, blackbird, thrush, and finch,
I'll sing enough for all you lazy kind!'

And when I hear him at this daring task,
'Peace, little bird,' I say, 'and take some rest;
Stop that wild, screaming fire of angry song,
Before it makes a coffin on your nest.'

W H Davies

April's charms

When April scatters coins of primrose gold
Among the copper leaves in thickets old,
And singing skylarks from the meadows rise,
To twinkle like black stars in sunny skies;

When I can hear the small woodpecker ring
Time on a tree for all the birds that sing;
And hear the pleasant cuckoo, loud and long –
The simple bird that thinks two notes a song;

When I can hear the woodland brook, that could
Not drown a babe, with all his threatening mood;
Upon whose banks the violets make their home,
And let a few small strawberry blossoms come.

When I go forth on such a pleasant day,
One breath outdoors takes all my care away;
It goes like heavy smoke, when flames take hold
Of wood that's green and fill a grate with gold.

W H Davies

Day's black star

Is it that small black star,
    Twinkling in broad daylight,
Upon the bosom of
    Yon cloud so white –
Is it that small black thing
Makes earth and all Heaven ring?

147

Sing, you black star; and soar
    Until, alas! too soon
You fall to earth in one
    Long swinging swoon;
But you will rise again
To Heaven, from this green plain.

Sing, sing, sweet star; though black,
    Your company's more bright
Than any star that shines
    With a white light;
Sing, Skylark, sing; and give
To me thy joy to live.

W.H. Davies

Song

There, sharp and sudden, there I heard –
Ah, some wild lovesick singing bird
Woke singing in the trees?
The nightingale and babble-wren
Were in the English greenwood then,
And you heard one of these?

The babble-wren and nightingale
Sang in the Abyssinian vale
That season of the year!
Yet, true enough, I heard them plain,
I heard them both, again, again,
As sharp and sweet and clear
As if the Abyssinian tree
Had thrust a bough across the sea,

Had thrust a bough across to me
With music for my ear!

I heard them both, and oh! I heard
The song of every singing bird
That sings beneath the sky,
And with the song of lark and wren
The song of mountains, moths and men
And seas and rainbows vie!

I heard the universal choir
The Sons of Light exalt their Sire
With universal song,
Earth's lowliest and loudest notes,
Her million times ten million throats
Exalt Him loud and long,
And lips and lungs and tongues of Grace
From every part and every place
Within the shining of His face,
The universal throng.

Ralph Hodgson
(1871–1962)

In Flanders fields

In Flanders fields the poppies blow
Between the crosses, row on row,
That mark our place; and in the sky
The larks, still bravely singing, fly,
Scarce heard amid the guns below.
We are the Dead. Short days ago
We lived, felt dawn, saw sunset glow,
Loved and were loved, and now we lie: .
      In Flanders fields.

Take up our quarrel with the foe:
To you from failing hands we throw
The torch; be yours to hold it high.
If ye break faith with us who die
We shall not sleep, though poppies grow
      In Flanders fields.

Lieut.-Col. John D. McCrae
(1872–1918)

Over Salève

Over Salève I heard a skylark singing
  Blessèd be Beauty, Beauty! He soared and swirled,
In very ecstasy of flight outflinging
  His breathless music on a broken world.
Joy, the sole faith of that so tiny flyer
  Twining unnumbered notes in psalms of praise,
Lifted him up on high and ever higher
  Till the blue heaven hid him from my gaze.

Still he adored, flooding the sky and mountain
  With delicate waves of sound more silver-sweet
Than the pure flowing of a pebbled fountain
  To desert-farers fainting in the heat.
Beggar am I for Beauty's least caress;
The little lark knows all her loveliness.

George Herbert Clarke
(1873–1953)

The skylark (*Alauda arvensis*)

During my life I have probably listened to more Larks singing than any other British songster. For me, nevertheless, this sweet-voiced minstrel has a special charm, and I should never tire of listening to its joyous melodies. I may say at once it is my favourite British song-bird; it has an attraction and a fascination indescribable, thus I may be pardoned perhaps if in my notes respecting the bird's song I may appear over-zealous in the praise bestowed upon this scorner of the ground.

The song itself is of so beautiful a description that any attempt to write it down must surely fail. As the bird proceeds in its aerial flights it seems to increase in volume, sweetness and cadence. Right unto its final outburst, just previous to the final fall to the earth, the bird appears to gather music as it goes. Albeit, the song seems little varied, yet it can never become monotonous! Its sweet chromatic lays and trills – call them what you will – uttered as they are during such prolonged and interesting song flights, always hold me entranced, and no sooner have I finished watching one particular bird alight safely on the ground, than I find myself eagerly scanning another bird just ascending and I have often been entertained for a whole morning in Lark-land alone.

My notes with regard to this feathered musician are very frequent, for the reason that no matter when I am in or near my house I can hear half a dozen of these birds pouring out their joyful melodies. They are very plentiful indeed in this part of Hertfordshire, but, alas for the Nature lover! the town is rapidly extending its area, and many an old green lane of my boyhood has been effaced beyond recognition. The expulsion of the Larks as neighbours of mine is, I am afraid, near at hand. A year or two will probably see them driven away from their present haunts, for by that time bricks and mortar will have superseded the cornfields, the meadow lands and the other rural surroundings, but 'sufficient unto the day is the evil thereof'.

The Lark's period of song is a lengthy one; it sings practically eleven months out of the twelve, and is, in my opinion, the most continuous song-bird in the British Isles. It is never affected by the weather; rain, snow, hail, heat, wind, all come alike to it, and it invariably sings with its head to the breeze.

How the Lark cleaves the air, especially when looked at through a pair of good glasses. Is it not interesting to watch it soaring upward? Taking the glass from the eye, the observer can scarcely see the bird again with the naked eye, as it towers higher and higher until finally lost in the blue sky. Then it suddenly commences the descent, falling slowly, slowly, slowly, singing all the while, until finally it drops to the earth in a slanting direction.

He who can hear a Lark sing without straining his eyes upwards to catch a sight of the blithe spirit, as Shelley so ably described the bird, must surely be one who 'hath no music in himself'. I should add that I have known the bird to sing for forty-five minutes at a stretch, soaring the whole time, and that I have seen it perch on trees, which is a contrary observation to that of most writers.

Besides being such an avid musician the Skylark is also of much service in regard to the insects, and obnoxious seeds it devours. It cannot be gainsaid, however, that it does not do harm to shooting corn. The late Grant Allen writes: 'At the same time that our own

152

birds thus scatter themselves in the cornfields, vast reinforcements of Continental Skylarks arrive for the winter. They seem to have bee driven out of their own breeding-places by severe weather, and to come to England in search of food, which they find abundantly in our hospitable stubbles. Here they search for seeds, and, as they live in great part off grains of noxious weeds, like black bindweed, knotweed, corn-poppy and couch grass, I believe they are really most useful friends of the agricultural interest. They also devour a certain number of hibernating insects, and as these are for the most part egg-bearing females, laden with the broods of the succeeding year, they doubtless render good service in this way also. It is urged, on the other hand, that Larks commit depredations on the stacks and corn yards in severe weather, and that they do damage to autumn-sown crops and young spring plants. This is no doubt true; but it is more than counterbalanced, not only in my opinion, but in that of many practical farmers, by the service they perform in destroying grubs and the seeds of noxious weeds. The farmer finds it no small advantage to have his stubble picked over, inch by inch, with ceaseless care, by a whole horde of eager and sharp-eyed assistants, who seldom pass by a single grain of the smaller plants which would otherwise eat up and absorb the nutriment he spreads upon the fields for the benefit of his corn crops.'

It is an active, engaging bird, both in the air and upon the ground.

The nesting season is April to June, though I have found a nest as late as July. It is generally placed in a hollow amongst standing grass or other herbage, often in the footprint of a cow, or quite close to a meadow path. Grass, with a lining of finer portions of the same, go to make up the nest. Four or five eggs are laid. These are whitish-grey, or yellowish, spotted and freckled, generally thickly, with darker grey, brown or dark yellow. Some I have seen nearly black and pointed, others nearly round and decidedly yellowish-brown.

I know of no local names for the bird, it is so universally known.

Above, the bird possesses three shades of brown, the darkest being along the shaft of each feather; over the eye is a faint streak of white; yellowish-white underneath with a brown tinge; dark brown spots on throat and neck sides, forming a gorget just above the breast.

W. Percival Westell
(1874–1943)

June

June, sunny June, is not only the month of roses, for, during the sixth month of the year, the young birds are very prominent along the countryside, and with the advent of the tiny fledglings, the songs of the male parent birds cease to a great extent. For this there is ample reason, as in all other things in the wonderful realm of Nature, if only we stop to make inquiries. The courtship season has by leafy June almost ceased, and the rivalry among the male birds has to a very great extent ended. Therefore, as birds' songs are, earlier in the year, a sort of vocal blandishment, it is not necessary that the beautiful lyrics which captivate the heart of the female should be uttered any longer.

One great exception must be chronicled in the case of the Skylark...

W. Percival Westell

from **On Moulsford Down**

I saw a skylark springing
  Into the morning light,
He mounted singing, singing
  Till he was out of sight;
Gone was the music bringer,
  But not what did belong,
For, though I'd lost the singer,
  I still could hear the song.

When I must quit the rhyming
  And throw the pen away,
May I go out a-climbing
  On just so glad a day,
And it go on without me,
  All sun and cloud and wind,
And someone say about me,
  'He leaves a song behind.'

Patrick R. Chalmers
(1875–1942)

Good-night

The skylarks are far behind that sang over the down;
I can hear no more those suburb nightingales;
Thrushes and blackbirds sing in the gardens of the town
In vain: The noise of man, beast, and machine prevails.

But the call of children in the unfamiliar streets
That echo with a familiar twilight echoing,
Sweet as the voice of nightingale or lark, completes
A magic of strange welcome, so that I seem a king.

Among man, beast, machine, bird, child, and the ghost
That in the echo lives and with the echo dies.
The friendless town is friendly; homeless, I am not lost;
Though I know none of these doors, and meet but
      strangers' eyes.

Never again, perhaps, after to-morrow, shall
I see these homely streets, these church windows alight,
Not a man or woman or child among them all:
But it is All Friends' Night, a traveller's good-night.

Edward Thomas
(1878–1917)

The Rosses

My sorrow that I am not by the little dún
By the lake of the starlings at Rosses under the hill,
And the larks there, singing over the fields of dew,
Or evening there, and the sedges still.
For plain I see now the length of the yellow sand,
And Lissadell far off and its leafy ways,
And the holy mountain whose mighty heart
Gathers into it all the coloured days.

My sorrow that I am not by the little dún
By the lake of the starlings at evening when all is still,
And still in whispering sedges the herons stand,
'Tis there I would nestle at rest till the quivering moon
Uprose in the golden quiet over the hill.

Seumas O'Sullivan
(1879–1958)

Lark's song

In Mercer Street the light slants down,
And straightway an enchanted town
Is round him, pinnacle and spire
Flash back, elate, the sudden fire,
And clear above the silent street
Falls suddenly and strangely sweet
The lark's song. Bubbling, note on note
Rise fountain-like, o'erflow and float
Tide upon tide, and make more fair
The magic of the sunlit air.
No more the cage can do him wrong,
All is forgotten save his song:
He has forgot the ways of men,
Wide heaven is over him again,
And round him the wide fields of dew
That his first infant morning knew,
E'er yet the dolorous years had brought
The hours of captive anguish, fraught
With the vile clamour of the street,
The insult of the passing feet,
The torture of the daily round,

The organ's blasphemy of sound.
Sudden some old swift memory brings
The knowledge of forgotten wings,
He springs elate and panting falls
At the rude touch of prison walls.
Silence. Again the street is grey;
Shut down the windows. Work-a-day.

Seumas O'Sullivan

Suicide in the trenches

I knew a simple soldier boy
Who grinned at life in empty joy,
Slept soundly through the lonesome dark,
And whistled early with the lark.

In winter trenches, cowed and glum,
With crumps and lice and lack of rum,
He put a bullet through his brain.
No one spoke of him again.

Siegfried Sassoon
(1879–1958)

The skylark caged

Beat, little breast, against the wires,
 Strive, little wings and misted eyes,
Which one wild gleam of memory fires
 Beseeching still the unfettered skies,
Whither at dewy dawn you sprang
Quivering with joy from this dark earth and sang.

And still you sing – your narrow cage
  Shall set at last your music free!
Its rapturous wings in glorious rage
  Mount and are lost in liberty,
While those who caged you creep on earth
Blind prisoners from the hour that gave them birth.

Sing! The great city surges round.
  Blinded with light, thou canst not know.
Dream! 'Tis the fir-woods' windy sound
  Rolling a psalm of praise below.
Sing, o'er the bitter dust and shame,
And touch us with thine own transcendent flame.

Sing, o'er the city dust and slime;
  Sing, o'er the squalor and the gold,
The greed that darkens earth with crime,
  The spirits that are bought and sold.
O, shower the healing notes like rain,
And lift us to the height of grief again.

Sing! The same music swells your breast,
  And the wild notes are still as sweet
As when above the fragrant nest
  And the wild billowing fields of wheat
You soared and sang the livelong day,
And in the light of heaven dissolved away.

The light of heaven! Is it not here?
  One rapture, one ecstatic joy,
One passion, one sublime despair,
  One grief which nothing can destroy,
You – though your dying eyes are wet,
Remember, 'tis our blunted hearts forget.

Beat, little breast, still beat, still beat,
  Strive, misted eyes and tremulous wings;
Swell, little throat, your Sweet! Sweet! Sweet!
  Thro' which such deathless memory rings:
Better to break your heart and die,
Than, like your jailers, to forget your sky.

Alfred Noyes
(1880–1958)

Sunshine and song

It was very hot.

Not a cloud showed in the blue sky – a blueness dulled by the heat so that the heaven was tinted like a starling's egg. The air in the park was heavy with the scent of hawthorn blossom; in the shade of the wide-spreading beeches the little fallow deer lay and twitched, flicked their ears and wagged their stumpy tails, for the flies tormented; above the drooping grasses and the croziers of the bracken there was a shimmering as the heat rays were flung back from the baked earth.

It was very hot.

From a distant clump of oaks there came the rapid rat-tat-tat of a drumming woodpecker – that curious noise which even today causes discussion among bird-lovers, some of whom say it is produced vocally, others that it is the result of the knocking of the beak on a dead branch. The hammering sound, whatever its origin, might have awakened a sleeping lark, for no sooner had it ceased than a little crested bird sprang into the still air and with spread tail and fluttering wings spiralled up, singing as it rose. Up it went, the liquid notes falling fast, a solitary speck in the glare of the open sky.

When well-nigh invisible it hovered, singing all the while. Then it dived swiftly for a distance, checked slightly and swung along on the level. Again it dived, again it straightened out. So it disported, each time nearer the earth and always pouring out its gladsome music. The last dive was songless. The bird came to rest and was lost to sight amid the herbage.

But not for long. Its song broke out anew, this time on the ground where, with drooped and fluttering wings, it serenaded its mate, close sitting on a nest of bents and grass cunningly placed beneath a tussock not very far away. She never stirred. She did not even glance his way. Her eyes were half-closed; now and again she opened her beak. She felt the heat.

As though aware of her unresponsiveness the cock bird flung himself into the air again. While he thus climbed and sang, the other slipped off the nest and ran a little way through the grass. She came to where the soil was bare. There she bathed, dusting herself with every appearance of enjoyment, rolling on her side and flinging the coarse grit over herself by movements of her wings.

The singer in the air dived swiftly at a tangent, one wing pointing earthwards, the other at a rakish angle. He landed as before, in silence, and ran towards the nest. For a moment he halted there and looked inside where lay four grey-brown eggs. It was as though he wondered if his mate had disappeared through the earth. Then he, too, ran towards the bare patch where she basked. Together. they dusted themselves.

It was very hot.

William Robinson Calvert
(1882–?)

from **The birds**

O let your strong imagination turn
The great wheel backward, until Troy unburn,
And then unbuild, and seven Troys below
Rise out of death, and dwindle, and outflow,
Till all have passed, and none has yet been there:
Back, ever back. Our birds still crossed the air;
Beyond our myriad changing generations
Still built, unchanged, their known inhabitations.
A million years before Atlantis was
Our lark sprang from some hollow in the grass,
Some old soft hoof-print in a tussock's shade...

Sir John Collings Squire
(1884–1958)

Shelley in the trenches

Impressions are like winds; you feel their cool
Swift kiss upon the brow, yet know not where
They sprang to birth: so like a pool
Rippled by winds from out their forest lair
My soul was stir'd to life; its twilight fled;
There passed across its solitude a dream
That wing'd with supreme ecstasy did seem;
That gave the kiss of life to long-lost dead.

A lark trill'd in the blue: and suddenly
Upon the wings of his immortal ode
My soul rushed singing to the ether sky
And found in visions, dreams, its real abode –
I fled with Shelley, with the lark afar,
Unto the realms where the eternal are.

Sgt. John William Streets
(1885–1916)

May

...At four o'clock (summer time) it is still dark. A few larks sing
faintly but only for a short while – a few cuckoo notes – and again
silence, till there grows an uncertain low twittering that suggests the
faint crackling of an ill-sustained heath fire. Again a silence, till at
five o'clock, the true dawn chorus grows to its full strength...

Elliott Lovegood Grant Watson
(1885–1970)

The skylark

The skylark may be called a bird of the field and of the sky, for its
nest is on the ground and a great deal of its life is spent warbling in
the sky almost out of sight.

All who have walked in the country across field, moor, heath or
hill must have watched the skylark climbing rapidly into the heavens,
singing as it goes. The skylark has solved the problem of rising
rapidly into the air, a problem which airmen have not solved so
successfully. The skylark rises in long slopes, with its wings

outstretched and its tail spread out almost like a fan. Up and up it goes in long spiral curves, at times almost vertically.

Poets who walk in the fields have watched the rising of the lark and have admired it. Nearly three hundred years ago, MILTON wrote –

> 'And now the herald lark
> Left his ground nest, high tow'ring to descry
> The morn's approach, and greet her with his song.'

Before this, SHAKESPEARE had heard the lark –

> 'Lo! here the gentle lark, weary of rest,
> From his moist cabinet mounts up on high,
> And wakes the morning, from whose silver breast
> The sun ariseth in majesty.'

Both these extracts form the writings of great poets remind us that a lark rises early, and one suggests that the best time to start the day's adventure is 'Up with the lark and away.'

We can hardly say that the lark has a song in the same sense as we speak of the song of the blackbird or the thrush. These two birds have a distinctive song, with clear-cut notes, whilst the lark's song is a twitter rather than a melody; yet some musicians with keen ear tell us that they can hear phrases of song repeated by the skylark that it must have heard from other birds. Several attempts have been made to put the twittering, bursting, ecstatic song of the lark into words. It cannot really be done, but here are two attempts which have been made.

(a) 'Cherry do, Cherry do, pretty joey, pretty joey, pretty
　　joey, white hat, white hat, pretty joey.'

(b) Written by a Scotsman –
　　'Up in the lift go we, te-hee, te-hee, te-hee!
　　There's no' a cobbler on the airth can make a shoe, to
　　　me, to me!
　　Why so? Why so? Why so?
　　Because my heel is as long as my toe!'

Do you notice any similarity between these?

The Scotsman, however, had not only listened to the song but he had also studied the bird. What does he say? 'My heel is as long as my toe.' If you get an opportunity to look at a lark's foot you will see that the toes are large and lie flat on the ground, and that the hind toe ends in a very long claw. You see that the heel is as long as the toe! This is the foot of a bird which lives on the ground and not amongst trees and bushes. Sometimes, it is true, the skylark does perch on a bough of a tree or on the top of a telegraph pole and almost burst itself in song, but these are exceptional times. The lark can both walk and run on the ground.

The nest of the lark is built on the ground, often in natural depression or in the footprint of a horse or cow that has walked in the field when it was soft. The outside of the nest is made of grass, and it is lined with moss, dry grass, rootlets and hair. The nest is extremely difficult to find, and in alighting the bird rarely lands near it. Sometimes the nest can be discovered by a kind of grass-run which leads to it. The skylark nests later than some birds, rarely laying its eggs before April. The grass is growing by this time, and frequently the nest is set amidst the growing corn, where the bird will be undisturbed. Before the corn is cut the babies will be hatched and away.

What size is the lark? Is it larger or smaller than a blackbird or a sparrow? Do you know?

Actually the lark is about seven inches long, whilst the blackbird is almost ten inches long. The house sparrow is only six inches in length. Both the male and the female are coloured alike, being brown in several shades, spotted and streaked so that either is difficult to see when quite still on the grass.

Camouflage. The eggs are a dirty yellowish white colour, spotted with olive brown, and four or five are usually laid in one clutch. The mother undertakes the task of sitting on the eggs, whilst the father hunts for food, feeds the family and sings the while.

It is true that larks do eat sprouting corn, tender shoots and seeds, but for the main part their food consists of worms, flies, caterpillars, and insects that are harmful to cultivated crops.

After the nesting season larks frequently gather in flocks and spend the autumn and winter together in search of food – another example of the gregarious habits of birds at times other than the breeding season. They sing almost all the year round, often finding company with skylarks which migrate from the colder continent in winter.

W.B. Little
(1888–?)

From the Somme

In other days I sang of simple things,
  Of summer dawn, and summer noon and night,
The dewy grass, the dew-wet fairy rings,
  The lark's long golden flight.

Deep in the forest I made melody
  While squirrels cracked their hazel nuts on high,
Or I would cross the wet sand to the sea
  And sing to sea and sky.

When came the silvered silence of the night
  I stole to casements over scented lawns,
And softly sang of love and love's delight
  To mute white marble fauns.

Oft in the tavern parlour I would sing
  Of morning sun upon the mountain vine,
And, calling for a chorus, sweep the string
  In praise of good red wine.

I played with all the toys the gods provide,
  I sang my songs and made glad holiday.
Now I have cast my broken toys aside
  And flung my lute away.

A singer once, I now am fain to weep.
  Within my soul, I feel strange music swell,
Vast chants of tragedy too deep – too deep
  For my poor lips to tell.

Leslie Coulson
(1889–1916)

Returning, we hear the larks

Sombre the night is:
And, though we have our lives, we know
What sinister threat lurks there.

Dragging these anguished limbs, we only know
This poison-blasted track opens on our camp –
On a little safe sleep.

photograph by Chris Knights

But hark! Joy – joy – strange joy.
Lo! Heights of night ringing with unseen larks:
Music showering on our upturned listening faces.

Death could drop from the dark
As easily as song –
But song only dropped,
Like a blind man's dreams on the sand
By dangerous tides;
Like a girl's dark hair, for she dreams no ruin lies there,
Or her kisses where a serpent hides.

Isaac Rosenberg
(1890–1918)

To a lark in war time

Hail to thee, blithe spirit!
Bird thou never wert – SHELLEY

Thou heavenly quivering beneath the deathlike above!
Thou ethereal whirring above the deadly beneath!
Thou ever prolific, prolific soul!
Oh hope, not ours,
In the midst of this tearless abyss!
We lift our hardened feet
To drums and convicts' march.
Trumpets, whips on the open flesh
Flog us and force us ahead.

Still we can feel thee aloft
Over our slavish necks,
Thee, little ardent one,
Thee, God's flamelet of song.

Oh thou life, thou innocent speck,
Thou art not of us!
Because we lie,
We bellow and glare
When the guard herds us to soup.
We fear just one thing,
Our master, the whip.
And so we are not what we are.

But thou, tiny lark,
Thou unblemished, exquisite truth,
Thou doest thy life,
Thou livest thy song, and
Thou art what thou art.

Franz Werfel
(1890–1945)

transl. from the German
by Edith Abercrombie Snow

A rainy day in April

When the clouds shake their hyssops, and the rain
Like holy water falls upon the plain,
'Tis sweet to gaze upon the springing grain
    And see your harvest born.

And sweet the little breeze of melody
The blackbird puffs upon the budding tree,
While the wild poppy lights upon the lea
   And blazes 'mid the corn.

The skylark soars the freshening shower to hail,
And the meek daisy holds aloft her pail,
And Spring all radiant by the wayside pale
   Sets up her rock and reel.

See how she weaves her mantle fold on fold,
Hemming the woods and carpeting the wold.
Her warp is of the green, her woof the gold,
   The spinning world her wheel.

Francis Ledwidge
(1892–1917)

Spring

Once more the lark with song and speed
Cleaves through the dawn, his hurried bars
Fall, like the flute of Ganymede
Twirling and whistling from the stars.

The primrose and the daffodil
Surprise the valleys, and wild thyme
Is sweet on every little hill,
When lambs come down at folding time.

In every wild place now is heard
The magpie's noisy house, and through
The mingled tunes of many a bird
The ruffled wood-dove's gentle coo.

Sweet by the river's noisy brink
The water-lily bursts her crown,
The kingfisher comes down to drink
Like rainbow jewels falling down.

And when the blue and grey entwine
The daisy shuts her golden eye,
The peace wraps all those hills of mine
Safe in my dearest memory.

Francis Ledwidge

A field in June

Greed is dumb at sight of so much gold
As these immaculate cups lightly hold,
Nor do we finger with fever'd covetous look
The smooth meandering silver of the brook.
Untaxable bounties entering the mind's eye
From deep meadow and diamond-dropping sky,
Wool-gathering clouds and contemplating trees
Casting palpable shade, those and these
Spell silence, till a skylark, newly risen,
Lets joy and desire out of the dark prison.

Gerald Bullett
(1893–1958)

The Somme Valley, June, 1917

Comrade, why do you weep?
Is it sorrow for a friend
Who fell, rifle in hand,
His last stand at an end?

The thunder-lipped grey guns
Lament him, fierce and slow,
Where he found his dreamless bed,
Head to head with a foe.

The sweet lark beats on high
For the peace of those who sleep
In the quiet embrace of earth:
Comrade, why do you weep?

Frank Prewett
(1893–1962)

Lark, larke, lev-er-ock...

lark, larke, lev-er-ock (Eng.),
lar-ick, ler-rik, lav-er-ock, (Scotch).

The Skylark, with some variation of colouring, leading some ornithologists to suppose that there may be more species than one, extends all through Europe to the Himalayas and China. The lark is heard near London in full song as it rises into the air, as early as the 14th February if the weather be fine. Between that time and the beginning of March they pair; they breed on the ground, laying four or five eggs, which are greenish, spotted with brown.

'Just when the larks and when the shepherds rise.'

Edward Lloyd

The first day of spring

Between the hedges I could see the Atlantic, white upflung bursts of waves, a mile away and below. Above my left shoulder the bare grey ash saplings of the hedge, with their dark brown cloven buds, rattled and swished in the south-west wind, which was blowing half a gale. Gulls drifted overhead, rocking and crooking their wings. The fields of plough and pasture, the trees and thatched roofs of the farm buildings below, the flock of yellow-hammers alighting and flitting along the ruddy twigs of dogwood and the young leaves of honeysuckle, the plants of foxglove, the lichens on the stone – all took light from the sky, and freed the thought-encumbered spirit. Air and sun and wind, these are the inspiration of life, the ancient source of renewal, whose inherited essence is the beauty in Man's mind. A lark singing, and another lark, many larks: and it seemed to me, in the beauty of that moment, that the inspiration of walls and pavement was false, bringing upon men the things of darkness.

The wind and the sun vibrate the tissues charged and impressed in ancient days: I am one with the sunlight, and the lark is my brother. These feet must not break the flapping arrow-shaped leaves of the wild arum, as I clamber over a dog-gap in the hedge to the open fields, for its hopes are my hopes under the wide sky.

Henry Williamson
(1895–1977)

Lark descending

A singing firework; the sun's darling;
    Hark how creation pleads!
Then silence: see, a small gray bird
    That runs among the weeds.

Edmund Blunden
(1896-1974)

Last song

All my songs are risen and fled away;
    (Only the brave birds stay);
All my beautiful songs are broken or fled.
    My poor songs could not stay
Among the filth and the weariness and the dead.

There was bloody grime on their light, white feathery wings,
    (Hear how that lark still sings),
And their eyes were the eyes of dead men that I knew.
    Only a madman sings
When half of his friends lie asleep for the rain and the dew.

The flowers will grow over the bones of my friends;
    (The birds' song never ends);
Winter and summer, their fair flesh turns to clay.
    Perhaps before all ends
My songs will come again that have fled away.

2nd Lt. Henry Lamont Simpson
(1897–1918)

175

The lark

Everyone knows the lark's sweet, continuous song, when the lark himself is a mere speck. Few know him on the ground, however, and most children are surprised to see that he is quite a big bird. He is brown, about as big as a thrush, and he often raises the feathers on his head, giving himself a little crest.

He builds his nest on the ground in a field or on a common. His eggs are dull white, mottled with brown.

Notice how sibilant his song is, full of S sounds – 'Sweeo, sweeo, sis, sis, sweeo, swis, sweeo?'

Enid Blyton
(1898–1968)

The skylark

The skylark usually rears two broods each season, the first being generally abroad by the 10th of June, but often earlier, and in fine seasons so soon as the middle of May. Each brood consists of four or five young, which are fed on insects. When the breeding season is over, Larks cease for a time to sing, and fly quietly about in pairs, or a few together, intent on recruiting their energies by the abundant food which they find in the stubble and grass fields...

The slaughter of Larks for food is a crying abuse. A London shop-front recently exhibited the painful sight of festoons of larks, with the notice attached, 'Special order, ten thousand larks, one and sixpence a dozen.' *The Echo* (March 1891) states that the London markets were at that time daily receiving more than twenty thousand to forty thousand larks, which arrived at Leadenhall Market every morning in sacks, and were sold to the dealers by the bushel measure. The trade is increasing rather than diminishing.

The Star newspaper, which also took some trouble to investigate the matter, wrote on April 4th, 1894: – 'When *The Star* man went to Leadenhall Market, and tried to find out from the chief salesman there how many larks came into London market, he met with a surprise. 'You can hardly strike an average,' he was told. 'Some weeks there may be none, and I have seen truck after truck on the Great Eastern loaded with nothing but larks (chiefly from Cambridge, Lincolnshire, and the Brighton Downs).'

The bird-catcher as well as the epicure is to blame. 'It has long been thought desirable,' says Mr W. L. Woodroffe, 'by all who wish not to see rural England deprived of its best songsters, that some restriction should be put on the trade of bird-catching…it is simply monstrous that dwellers in London and other towns should have it in their power to send out and take birds by the million every year, to gratify a taste for caged songsters, most of which are doomed to perish after a few days of miserable captivity.' (W. L. Woodroffe, Leaflet No. 12, Society for the Protection of Birds.)

WORKERS ON THE GROUND

Food of the skylark throughout the year

	By eating which he benefits man.	By eating which he robs man.
January	Insects, seeds of weeds, worms; in hard weather, leaves, waste roots, etc., in fallow lands.	
February	Seeds of weeds, insects, waste grain, succulent leaves.	
March	Insects, worms, grubs, seeds of weeds. Wire-worms, etc., on newly-ploughed lands.	Seed corn, but seldom to any serious extent.
April	Beetles, insects, wire-worms, eggs of insects. Green food.	Sprouting corn, if not deeply sown

May	Beetles, ants and their eggs, grubs of turnip-moth (Agrotis segetum). Surface grubs of all kinds.	
June	Flies, grubs, and insects of all kinds, seeds of chickweed, plantain, knotgrass, etc. Seeds of wild grasses.	
July	Surface caterpillars, grass-hoppers, worms, weevils, ants and their eggs. Wireworms.	A little corn.
August	Crickets, grasshoppers; flies, caterpillars, and grubs; chrysalids; wireworms.	A little corn.
September	Insects; seeds of weeds, such as charlock, etc.; the daddy-longlegs on the wing. Waste corn.	Seed corn, but not often to any great extent.
October	Worms, seeds of weeds; gleaned oats, barley, corn, etc., in stubble fields; berries.	
November	Seeds of weeds, waste corn in stubble; insects hidden in stubble, worms, chrysalids, eggs of insects.	
December	Seeds of weeds; worms, chrysalids; eggs of insects.	In hard weather, leaves of swedes and rape, and other vegetation appearing above the snow.

ABOUT THE SKYLARK'S FOOD

Weevils (*Sitones*, etc.). The highly-destructive insects called Weevils are distinguished from other beetles chiefly by their long snouts or beaks. They are the more capable of mischief on account of their small size and vast numbers. It is in the larval or grub stage that most weevils do their worst, but several of those which, like the pine weevil, infest trees, are terribly destructive at all stages. Corn, fruit-trees, vegetables, clover, grasses, alike suffer; in fact there is hardly any plant or tree useful to man that does not suffer from the ravages of its own special weevil, a large proportion of them being naturalised, not native, insects.

The small Grey and Brown Weevils classed together under the title *Sitones* are among the greatest enemies with which the farmer, gardener, and maltster have to deal. As regards the attacks of one species, *Sitones lineatus*, the Striped Clover Weevil, Curtis says:– 'These weevils, which sometimes swarm to an extraordinary amount in clover fields, completely riddle the leaves, reducing them to skeletons.' It would appear to be a second brood of this insect which in summer turns its attention to clover and lucerne. Peas and broad beans are equally to its taste earlier in the year.

Of the Purple Clover Weevil (*Apion apricans*), the female of which lays her eggs in the clover blossoms he adds, 'Some idea may be formed of the ravages occasioned by this weevil by the following communication made to me by Mr William Thenchard of Sherborne: – 'I have a field of clover which has been twice mown, and there is now a fine aftermath. The part of the field near the stack has been lately attacked by a small black weevil which advances in a semi-circle, totally destroying every leaf, leaving only the fibre. I should think there are on some of the leaves as many as a hundred or a hundred and fifty. Since last night they have eaten as much as would have kept a sheep. They destroy every leaf in their progress'. Lime, salt, soot, etc., does not injure them.'

The mother weevil of *Sitones lineatus* lays her eggs, it is supposed, on the ground, for the grubs of clover weevils are generally found feeding at the roots of the clover. The perfect beetles feed standing on the edge of the leaf like caterpillars, and feeding inwards. When the *Sitones lineatus* weevil directs its energies to young peas and beans, the perfect weevils cause marks which

179

resemble those which might be left by the beak of a bird. Sparrows .and other birds which frequent the rows for the sake of devouring the insects are often accused by ignorant observers of causing the very harm which they come to prevent.

The *Sitones* weevils feed by day in full sunshine but the Rev. T. Wood states that he has watched them by the light of a lantern feeding by night. Dropping from the leaf on the least alarm, the weevils sham death lying still on the ground with legs tucked in. In this state they look so exactly like little dry grains of earth that no eye but that of a bird could distinguish them. As soon as they consider the danger to be past, they run up the stem and begin to feed again.

Writing to Curtis, a farmer says, ' I have searched a long time for them in vain in fields where they were committing their ravages, in order to convince my neighbours what they were indebted to for the loss of their crops. I have a field of peas that swarms with them at this time, the remaining leaves of which are quite riddled. When a person walks in amongst them you may hear a pattering like rain upon the leaves occasioned by their dropping down'. The perfect weevil hides during winter in stubble-stems and similar places, coming out occasionally, however. It hibernates in the pupa or chrysalis stage also. Immense numbers of them have been observed scattered in a torpid state over the surface of the snow.

The services of the Skylark, which not only feeds himself and brings up his young ones among the growing crops in summer, but also hungrily searches the stubbles for insects in winter, must be enormous in keeping such creatures in check. The small quantity of corn which a skylark pilfers cannot be weighed against the waste and ruin wrought by even one *Sitones* Weevil and its progeny.

OPINIONS OF AUTHORITIES

Countless Insects and Seeds. – 'Larks must consume an enormous number of the seeds of pernicious weeds. They also, during summer months, and, indeed, during most of the year, destroy a vast quantity of insects. Larks are very fond of frequenting hollows and newly-ploughed fields, where they cannot do any damage, and must consume countless insects and seeds of weeds turned up by the plough and cultivator.' ('*Ornithology and Agriculture*,' p 156, paper by O. V. Aplin, F.L.S., Member of the British Ornithologists Union.)

A Hint to Farmers. – 'The skylarks food consists of small insects and seeds, which it collects among the herbage of stubble-fields, meadows, and downs, or in newly-ploughed fields. To this fare it adds, in winter and spring, the tender stalk of sprouting corn. Hence it is regarded with deadly hostility by farmers. Farmers would effect a great saving if they sowed their wheat deeper than is the usual practice. The only part of the young plant which the lark touches is the white stalk between the grain and the blade. In its effort to obtain this, it frequently destroys the whole plant, if the grain has been lodged near the surface: but if the young shoot have sprouted from a depth of an inch or more, the bird contents itself with as much as it can reach without digging, and leaves the grain uninjured, and capable of sprouting again.' (*British Birds in their Haunts*, Rev. C. A. Johns)

Weeds and Wireworms. – 'The food of the skylark is composed, to some extent, of farm produce, but for this it makes amends by eating many destructive insects, including the wireworm, as well as the seeds of such pernicious weeds as charlock, knotgrass, and chickweed. Seed corn, especially autumn-sown wheat, both before and after sprouting, possesses great attractions for it, but it is only in exceptional cases that the crop is materially injured by it. It should be remembered that the wireworm is known to enter into the skylark's dietary, and, when a crop fails to *braird* (*i.e.* shoot up) thickly, it is advisable to make quite certain of the cause before accusing the birds.' ('Wild Birds, Useful and Injurious,' C. F. Archibald, *Journal of Royal Agricultural Society*, No. 17, March 1894, p 73.)

Threatened Extermination in France. – 'This family (the larks) renders eminent service to agriculturists by the enormous quantities of worms, caterpillars, and grasshoppers it devours. The season of incubation over, larks assemble in numerous flocks, having now only their food to think; of, and that being plentiful they soon get plump and fat. In countries like France, this is the signal for their destruction, for persons assemble in all quarters to make a raid on these valuable innocents, using every means to accomplish their work of death; and unless the legislature interferes on their behalf by passing laws for their preservation, the race will probably be exterminated in that country.' ('Reptiles and Birds' Figuier, p 502, date 1892, revised edition.)

Cruel Caging. – 'The persecution to which the lark is subjected, unfortunately for itself, is not due to its occasional robberies alone, for there are two other causes which annually lead to its capture in immense numbers. The first of these is the well-known song of the bird, which brings it into great request among the bird-fanciers, and so proves a curse rather than a blessing to its owner. To condemn a lark to life-long imprisonment is, perhaps, a greater cruelty than to treat any other bird in a similar manner, for its delight in freedom is so great that one cannot but pity it intensely when deprived of all that made life pleasant to it, and doomed to fret away its existence within the bars of its narrow cage. Yet one has only to pass through the centres of the bird-fancying fraternity to realise to how great an extent this cruelty is carried on.' (*'Our Bird Allies,'* Rev. T. Wood, p. 186.)

Shameful Epicurism. – 'The remaining cause for the persecution of the bird is, of course, the great demand for it as a dainty for the epicure's table: and, in order to supply this demand, thousands upon thousands of larks are sometimes trapped in a single locality in a single day. Against this traffic there is less to be said, for the birds are captured for a real, if luxurious object, and are killed at once, instead of being subjected to months or years of wearisome and hopeless imprisonment. The fact, however, remains that thousands upon thousands of a useful bird are annually killed for a practically needless purpose, and agriculturists injured to no little degree by the consequent loss of their services.'

Edith Carrington

The lark above the trenches

'A French soldier writing to *Le Matin* says that the other day a lark sang above the trenches its spring song, which was to them a song of joy and hope.' – February 1915

> All day the guns had worked their hellish will,
>   And all night long
> With sobbing breath men gasped their lives away,
> Or shivered restless on the ice-cold clay,
>   Till morn broke pale and chill
>   With sudden song.
>
> Above the sterile furrows war had ploughed
>   With deep-trenched seams,
> Wherein this year such bitter seed is sown,
> Wherein this year no fruitful grain is strown,
>   A lark poured from the cloud
>   Its throbbing dreams.

It sang – and pain and death were passing shows –
    So glad and strong;
Life soared triumphant, though a myriad men
Were swept like leaves beyond the living's ken,
    That wounded hope arose
    To greet that song.

Muriel Elsie Graham

The lark at heaven's gate

You will note that we are approaching a turn in the lane – for the longest lane has a turning – and that on the right is the stile I told you of. Christian and Hopeful (as you remember) forsook the road for a meadow; and, having climbed on a stile, they found themselves in a very pleasant world till presently Giant Despair laid hands upon them, flinging them into a dungeon of Doubting Castle. Nevertheless, we will turn our backs on the lane and step into the field at the other side of the hedge, rejoicing, you and I, to have buttercups and daisies about our feet, and larks carolling far overhead.

Larks! Poets and philosophers have been stirred by the skylark which, singing still dost soar, and soaring ever singest, as Percy Bysshe Shelley says so finely...Let us, then listen to the lark this morning, even though we did not rise with him, for he is the messenger of the day.

Up in a morning early is the lark, it seems, and I confess that that is where he scores a point over me, for among my virtues is *not* that of rising early. Still, I admire those who do, and none deserves adulation more than this ethereal minstrel, this heart-throb of the sky. No wonder that an old Sussex philosopher once said:

The man who kills a skylark shows
How far from God man sometimes goes.

184

Oliver J. Pike, in one of his charming books writes something like this: 'Higher and higher he rises, his notes sounding weaker as he nears the fleecy clouds. At last the singer reaches his limit, flutters and struggles to get higher, but strength fails, although he still sings, resting on the outspread wings; and then he descends.

'The pure notes go straight to my heart and fill me with joy. Down, down he comes – still slowly – and singing as if his little body could not contain the joy and thanksgiving he is pouring out so passionately and fully. Halfway down he stops, flutters, and tries to soar again, but he cannot.

'What memories the notes awaken! A spell holds me as this little harbinger of spring heralds brighter days.'

On wings of song rises the lark, and in England – as also in parts of Scotland – one may hear a score of larks singing together at heaven's gate. Perhaps we are too fortunate, and therefore think but little of this marvellous bird which makes a nest and lays its eggs in the ground, yet climbs to such dizzy heights.

Let us, then, remind ourselves that not every region of the earth has a lark population such as ours. It was in 1912 that a whole load of living English birds was sent to Canada. They arrived safely, and were set free in one of the parks of Victoria, British Columbia. In their first winter all the birds perished except two – a pair of skylarks which, one sunny spring day in 1913, were heard singing about two miles from the spot where they had been liberated. Folk stopped to look up and listen, and the newspapers of Victoria carried headlines announcing that English larks had been heard in the town. Since then, happily, the larks have multiplied amazingly, and now, go where you will on Vancouver Island, you will hear the larks trilling in the blue.

Proudly do I remember that at Hawkes Ridge Aerodrome, Buckinghamshire, flew two Union Jacks a month or two before the Second World War. Bravely they fluttered in the breeze and pilots about to descend were careful never to taxi along the ground *between* the two flags. Why? All because a lark had a nest there, and was rearing her family where the tyres of a plane might crush the youngsters to death.

ALL'S WELL THAT ENDS WELL

But I must tell you about the skylarks that caused a stir in Ipswich not long ago. In the middle of a meadow on the outskirts of town was a lark's nest. The mother-bird was well pleased, no doubt, with the site of her desirable residence, for the grass was thick, and no one ever crossed the meadow. There she laid her eggs. There her little ones were hatched. Life went merrily as a marriage bell.

Then, one day, came an invasion. The gate of the field was lifted from its hinges. Men by the score were tramping in. Lorries bumped over the grass, the noise of their engines terrifying the mother lark and her startled brood. Huge tents were erected. There was much hammering and shouting. No wonder the little mother fluttered anxiously over her nest, expecting every moment that the wheel of a lorry or the heel of a workman would destroy all she loved most. How in the world could she have foreseen that the Royal Show of Ipswich was to be held in *that* field?

Now there was in the field a valuable Jersey cow, and the cow was tended by a kindly herdswoman. She saw the frightened mother lark. She heard her cries. So she either begged, borrowed, or stole a bit of sacking and a few sticks, and erected in the middle of the great exhibition the smallest tent of all – a kind of rude wigwam – above the lark's nest. Odd it was to see in the Jersey Ring this flimsy tent; but everyone knew why it was there – the herdswoman saw to that – and though cows and herdsman and judges and ring-stewards, and I know not who besides, walked within a few inches of the nest, no harm came to the mother bird or her brood.

186

The show lasted a week. Then came men with lorries to carry away the apparatus that had been used. Round the tent were placed protective hurdles; but somebody removed the hurdles without knowing why they were there, and a driver backed his lorry so that one of the wheels hung over the nest. This menace so terrified the mother lark that for a time she flew away, but the kindly herdswoman came to the rescue of the baby birds, feeding them with milk. Presently a crowd of men and boys gathered round the lorry, contriving to move it a few inches without the wheel crushing the nest.

Next day the herdswoman had to drive her Jersey cow home but before she left, she put up a notice in the field: WARNING: LARK'S NEST. Finally, the nest became the responsibility of the local Fire Brigade.

So the Ipswich Royal Show came and went, and one day a man put the gate on its hinges again, and the lark and her fledglings enjoyed sole possession of the field.

FATHER ANSELM

Have you ever paused at the end of a summer day to let the magic of the country sink into your soul? Have you stood, say in your garden or in a meadow, the sun gone down, the hush of evening over all things, the beauty and serenity undisturbed till, suddenly, a late lark leaps from the ground, rises into the golden upper air, pours upon your wondering head a cataract of liquid melody and then falls back into the dewy shadows and a stillness that speaks of God? This I have known. It is an experience which always brings to mind W.E. Henley's fine poem beginning: *A late lark twitters from the quiet skies*, and ends;

So be my passing!
My task accomplished and the long day done,
My wages taken, and in my heart
Some late lark singing,
Let me be gathered to the quiet west,
The sundown splendid and serene,
Death.

And I must bring to your recollection one more word about a lark, that very old legend of a monk who, having wandered into the fields one summer morning, stood still to hear a lark sing for the first time in his life. He was entranced. Looking up, he watched the singing speck soaring into the blue; he drank the music of its song, and then returned to the monastery.

But when he would have entered, a doorkeeper he did not know bade him wait. The doorkeeper asked his name, and when the monk replied that he was Father Anselm, the doorkeeper shook his head, saying no monk of that name belonged to the monastery. Other monks came, all strangers to Father Anselm. At last, having consulted their records, they discovered that a certain Father Anselm had been a member of that fraternity *a hundred years before*.

Time, it seems, had been blotted out while Father Anselm had listened to the lark.

How fantastic the tale, yet how profoundly true!

H.L. Gee
(1901–1977)

Maytime in the Camargue

The reed-beds of Barbegal were alive with warblers; we heard the grasshopper-like song of the Savi's warbler as well as the great reed and reed warblers. Attractive and shy bearded tits popped up to have a look around occasionally and well in from our track was a heronry of purple herons.

Both short-toed and calendra larks were on the Entressen road, and on the Le Crau proper we were in a veritable land of larks. Skylarks everywhere reminded me of home. Did I merely imagine that they sang with even more *joie de vivre* than in Cornwall or did the challenge of greater numbers spur them on to greater endeavour?

Gail Carter Lott
(1903–1994)

189

The ecstatic

LARK, skylark, spilling your rubbed and round
Pebbles of sound in air's still lake,
Whose widening circles fill the noon; yet none
Is known so small beside the sun:

Be strong your fervent soaring, your skyward air!
Tremble there, a nerve of song!
Float up there where voice and wing are one,
A singing start, a note of light!

Buoyed, embayed in heaven's noon-wide reaches –
For soon light's tide will turn – oh stay!
Cease not till day streams to the west, then down
That estuary drop down to peace.

C. Day Lewis
(1904–1972)

February 16...

The solemn still weather continues, windless and misty, very like those days we get in early autumn but without any sense of autumn in the air, a sort of waiting for the spring. Walking along a little country road with daughter Angela she put her hand on my arm and said 'a lark'. I could hear nothing, yet that lark was singing vigorously, a song which was at one time one of my favourites and now, to my sorrow, I cannot hear it! But I could see it, mounting its invisible steps to heaven as though drawn up in jerks like a marionette.

As a boy I was entranced by the rising singing larks. Lying on my back on the Rectory lawn at Lamport I would watch the bird as it went. The greatest magic for me was to hear that song dwindling fainter and fainter until the bird was a mere speck high above the earth. I watched the lark this morning until it was lost to sight, but even so Angela, with her young ears, could hear it still. How I envied her!

Then I saw a falling speck. It was dropping like a stone within twenty feet or less of the field when it opened its wings and finished the flight with a long sweeping glide. No wonder the lark has attracted the attention of poets, indeed this habit of soaring high into the sky is shared with no other British bird.

'B.B.' (Denys James Watkins-Pitchford)
(1905–1990)

That continuous trilling music...

...No wonder poets waxed lyrical about the lark for there is something about that continuous trilling music becoming fainter and fainter as the bird ascends, which is strangely moving. I remember watching and listening to that faint (and fainter) music until the bird itself was out of sight, but still there came down to me a tiny silver stream of sound.

'B.B.' (Denys James Watkins-Pitchford)

The earliest art...

...The earliest art was inspired by animals. It has been suggested by a Hungarian musicologist, Szoke, that the first musical scales were imitated from bird song, and W.H. Thorpe believes that the suggestion is plausible. The fundamental intervals of bird song and human song are the same. While for the bird this is the result of its vocal equipment, there is nothing in man's which necessitates it. 'It seems highly plausible that the intervals which are acceptable to the human ear, as normal and natural for music, are in fact those intervals which were first offered to the ancestors of man by bird song. Since man always had bird song all around, impinging on his ears, is it not reasonable to suppose that he developed a musical signal system by imitating the birds? This bird-song was palaeo-melody. Human pre-music gradually developed, according to this theory, to be the component of the total art of primitive society and later to be differentiated musical art.'

Diana Spearman
(1905–1991)

Perception

While I have vision, while the glowing-bodied,
Drunken with light, untroubled clouds, with all this cold
    sphered sky,
Are flushed above trees where the dew falls secretly,
Where no man goes, where beasts move silently,
As gently as light feathered winds that fall
Chill among hollows filled with sighing grass;

While I have vision, while my mind is borne
A finger's length above reality,
Like that small plaining bird that drifts and drops
Among these soft lapped hollows;
Robed gods, whose passing fills calm nights with sudden
    wind,
Whose spears still bar our twilight, bend and fill
Wind-shaken, troubled spaces with some peace,
With clear untroubled beauty;
That I may rise not chill and shrilling through perpetual day,
Remote, amazèd, larklike, but may hold
The hours as firm, warm fruit,
This finger's length above reality.

Peter Courtney Quennell
(1905–1994)

Splendour on the links

How straight it flew, how long it flew,
  It clear'd the rutty track
And soaring, disappeared from view
  Beyond the bunker's back –
A glorious, sailing, bounding drive
That made me glad I was alive.

And down the fairway, far along
  It glowed a lonely white;
I played an iron sure and strong
  And clipp'd it out of sight,
And spite of grassy banks between
I knew I'd find it on the green.

And so I did. It lay content
  Two paces from the pin;
A steady putt and then it went
  Oh, most securely in.
The very turf rejoiced to see
That quite unprecedented three.

Ah! seaweed smells from sandy caves
  And thyme and mist in whiffs,
In-coming tide, Atlantic waves
  Slapping the sunny cliffs,
Lark song and sea sounds in the air
And splendour, splendour everywhere.

John Betjeman
(1906–1984)

Allotments: April

Cobbled with rough stone which rings my tread
The path twists through the squared allotments.
Blinking to glimpse the lark in the warming sun,
In what sense am I joining in
Such a hallooing, rousing April day,
Now that the hedges are so gracious and
Stick out at me moist buds, small hands, their opening
      scrolls and fans?

Lost to some of us the festival joy
At the bursting of the tomb, the seasonal mystery,
God walking again who lay all winter
As if in those long barrows built in the fields
To keep the root-crops warm. On squires' lawns
The booted dancers twirl. But what I hear
Is spade slice in pebbled earth, swinging the nigger-coloured
      loam.

And the love-songs, the mediaeval grace,
The fluting lyrics, 'The only pretty ring-time',
These have stopped singing. For love detonates like sap
Up into the limbs of men and bears all the seasons
And the starving and the cutting and hunts terribly through
      lives
To find its peace. But April comes as
Beast-smell flung from the fields, the hammers, the loud-
      speaking weir.

Charles Bernard Spencer
(1909–1963)

The birds

Brother Thrush it was began
Matins for the dawn of man.
Brother Falcon watched him climb
Blindly from the depths of time,
Watched him till the earth, and bend
Fire and water to his end.
Brother Eagle, over all,
Heard the towering forests fall,
Saw the cities come and go
On the shifting world below.

Brother Gull suspended there
On the noiseless waves; of air,
Saw him ride the waves of sea
Buoyantly, triumphantly.
Brother Plover heard him rise
Thunderous towards the skies,
Saw the smooth projectiles follow
Brother Hawk and Brother Swallow,
And the mushroom cloudbursts grow
On the wasted world below.

Rooks in their high parliament
Say men to destruction sent
Bird and beast and fish, and then
Turned their hatred on to men.

Till they squandered equally
Air and fire, land and sea;
But, they say, when ages on
Men and all their works have gone,
Brother Lark will sing for them
His exultant Requiem.

Clive Sansom
(1910–1981)

The skylark and her enemy

There are a great many larks near our home. They sing so gaily in the morning as we go to school. But they sing much earlier than that.

We wanted once to try if we could get up before the lark. So we agreed to meet at five o clock in the morning, in the meadow where one has been singing all this year. We heard him before we got out of the lane. There he was, rising up into the air, going a little to the right, and then a little to the left, rising and singing all the time, as if he wanted to wake all the world with joy .

We watched him till he was quite a tiny speck in the sky. Then he came down again. When he was only a few feet from the ground he shut his wings and dropped into the grass.

The next morning we went at four o clock. That lark was not singing, but one in the next field was rising up as gay as a lark could be. Then our mothers said we must not get up any earlier. So we could not rise before the larks.

We caught a lark once to look at it, and then let it fly away again. It is not a gay bird. It has brown wings marked with dark streaks. Its breast and throat are a dull white, dotted with brown spots, and it has a white streak above its eye. Its feet are curious. The toes lie flat on the ground, and the hind toe has a very long claw. If you watch a lark you will see that he runs, he does not hop. Neither does he perch in the trees, and only sometimes on a low bush. He lives on the ground, except when he rises up to sing.

In the winter, as we go to school, we see large flocks of larks in the fields, looking for insects, and seeds of wheat and oats. When we come near them, they get up, a few at a time, and fly a little further. Then they wheel round and settle down to feed.

In the winter they scarcely ever sing. It is in the spring, when they pair, that they sing so beautifully.

About March we can often find a lark's nest hidden in the grass. They build in a rut, or a little hollow in the ground, often in the middle of the field. They line the nest with dry grass, and lay four or five eggs in it. The eggs are a dirty grey colour with brown spots on them, and they lie very snugly in the thick tufts of grass.

When the lark comes down after singing he does not drop close to the nest but a little way off. Then he runs up to the nest through the grass. This is because he is afraid that the sparrow-hawk might see the nest, and pounce on the little ones.

The sparrow-hawk is the lark's great enemy. One day we were looking at a lark rising up, and all at once we saw a sparrow-hawk just going to pounce upon it. The lark saw him too, and darted up faster than the hawk could soar. Then the hawk flew away a little and hovered about till the lark was tired and was obliged to come down. Then once more the hawk tried to pounce. But the lark was too clever for him. He closed his wings and dropped right down into the thick grass, and the hawk could not find him. We were glad the little lark was safe, and got back to his wife and little ones.

Arabella B. Buckley

198

Skylark

To me the lark's clear carolling on high
Reveals the whole wide blue, bright sky. – Anon.

The Skylark has always been one of the birds best loved by poets. It does indeed seem to belong more to heaven than to earth being the only British bird which sings while ascending, keeps singing while hovering and continues to sing while descending. He is a firework in the sky but, on the ground, just a nondescript grey-brown bird that runs among the stubble.

Happily, the Skylark is found wherever there is open country, whether it be cultivated land, saltings by the sea, heathery moors or the rolling downs. The bird is now the most widely distributed of any British species, since changes in farming methods with bigger fields and fewer hedgerows have suited it. The Skylark has no need of a songpost to establish his territory – all he needs is air.

How strange that the sun's darling, so celebrated in English poetry, is seen across the Channel as an important sporting bird. In EEC laws on bird protection the French have insisted on the right to continue shooting Skylarks. What makes it worse is that thousands of the larks are British-bred birds moving south in the autumn. It is a blessing that the Skylark is a highly adaptable species well able to hold its own.

Robert Dougal
(1913–   )

199

Poem in October

...A springful of larks in a rolling
Cloud and the roadside bushes brimming with whistling
Blackbirds and the sun of October
Summery
on the hill's shoulder,
Here where fond climates and sweet singers suddenly
Come in the morning where I wandered and listened
to the rain wringing
Wind blow cold
In the wood faraway under me...

Dylan Marlais Thomas
(1914–1953)

Song

Larks are the sparks
  Torn from the revolving earth
As it turns like a wheel through the night.

Larks are the sound
  To which silence is echo:
From their throat flows the river of light.

Larks are the dance
  In which the dancer is still –
Finding the perfect pose for their restless will.

200

Larks are the form
  To which all movement moves,
Sculpture bends, and music sings.
  They have such grace they fly from us;
  They are God's grace with wings!

Ronald Duncan
(1914–1982)

The sky-lark

A bird not distantly related to the Finches and Buntings is the Sky-Lark. This familiar species is one of the commonest birds of British cornfields. Everyone who has walked in the countryside in spring or early summer must have noticed the Larks leaping up from the fields and soaring on quivering pinions, pouring out their silver song as they rise. On a June day, England must be bathed in Sky-lark song, from Northumberland to Cornwall.

Yet, although the song seems to be continuous and although the birds seem to ascend clean out of sight, individual Sky-larks do not stay aloft for more than a few minutes. As soon as they have reached the crest of their climb they begin to descend, dropping in giant aerial steps and singing as they come.

Entirely birds of open country, Sky-larks are most at home in big arable fields, where they may nest among the growing corn and sing to a wide, windswept landscape. I have seen Sky-larks singing from a fence-post and also from the top of a small bush but never from a tree. The nesting of the Sky-lark is later than that of many other of the small birds of the countryside and therefore seldom falls foul of the spring operations on arable land, such as rolling, harrowing, and the sowing of chemical fertilisers. When these tasks are finished, the farmer is off the land for the few months to harvest, and it is during that period that the Sky-lark brings off a couple or even three broods. Consequently the Sky-lark population does not diminish.*

The reputation of the Sky-lark varies in different parts of the country. In the South-west, for instance, it seems to bear quite a good name and is seldom interfered with. In East Anglia, on the other hand, farmers accuse it of eating newly sown autumn grain. They say that the culprits are chiefly the immense hordes of Sky-larks which usually arrive on our eastern shores in autumn, and there seems to be some truth in this contention.

In general, Dr. W.E. Collinge gives the Sky-lark's food as 54% vegetable and 46% animal. The vegetable portion includes the seeds of many weeds and the leaves of plants such as clover, as well as grain. The animal part of the menu consists of insects, worms, slugs, millipedes and other small fry, most of them harmful to the farmer. The Royal Society for the Protection of Birds claims that, as regards food, the Sky-lark is 80% beneficial, 7% neutral and 13% harmful. With the possible exception of the east coast, where it is unfortunate that the arrival or these hosts of immigrants coincides with the autumn sowing, we may accept this as reasonably correct.

'Lark-pie' used to be a well-known rural dish, and larks are still appreciated by gourmets. The Sky-lark suffers little nowadays from the activities of people hoping to eat it, however.

The Wood-lark, near cousin to the Sky-lark, has an almost entirely insectivorous diet, but, as it prefers park-like or heath country away from agricultural land, these propensities are of little use to the farmer.

Ralph Whitlock
(1914-)

*Ralph Whitlock points out that this was a statement made in 1952. Since then, there has been a very serious diminution in the Sky-lark population. (Ed.)

A skylark and a merlin

...A friend of mine has rung to tell. me while walking on Exmoor he saw a most interesting encounter between a skylark and a merlin. One would naturally expect a small bird like a lark to be an easy prey for such an efficient killing machine as this hawk, but. this underestimates the lark's ability. Apparently in this case, the lark knew that its great weapon was the ability to climb very rapidly. This it did with the merlin in hot pursuit – higher and higher they went with the lark concentrating on climbing and not attempting to dodge in any way. Gradually the merlin's wing-beats got slower and slower until finally it had to abandon the chase, and dive away frustrated. A little exercise in the 'survival of the fittest'. That lark would perpetuate in its offspring the remarkable powers of vertical flight that characterise the species...

Bob Holmes
(1915–1994)

Sic transit gloria mundi

Come, break your heart, then, with the world's beauty
that so eludes you, though you be so close,
your breast upon the soil, where through the grasses
the long line of the little hillock grows,
and elms enormous hold the heavy sky up
and immemorial lark song scatters down
the pomp of summer morning, and swells more loud.

But when the long lanes of the evening light
lead through the willowy arrowed wood
to the perfection of sensory night
ah! the heart hungers, that this might forever
linger, the sudden stillness after sparrows
until the cricket sings, and your frail cry
be true that beauty will not fail
and all this glory will not die.

James Wreford Watson
(1915–   )

Prayers in a field

Like a handful of grain the words of blessing scatter
Over the cornfield. The callow heads of choirboys
Blond as dandelion cotton are ruffled by the wind,
And round their legs in a magpie whirl of black
And white plumage, cassock and surplice struggle,
Then everything holds its breath. A horse looks up
With mild, long cello face. A calf as red
As rusty iron chews over the day's cud

204

In this green evening. And then, like an upblown leaf
A lark twists, trembles, unfurls in crystal singing,
Bright notes, sharp facets, like rain-washed poplar leaves.
Upwards, onwards it flies, with the little rags
And tags and cotton ends of our thoughts and prayers,
Our humble, pitiful words clinging, as tufts
Of dandelion clutch at the passer-by.
How clean, how sure is that simplicity
Of a bird's song! And yet, in the ear of God
Which rings more clearly, that or the halting words
Of man, whose fallible breath is warm with love?

Margaret Stanley-Wrench
(1916–?)

The skylark

Wherever you find lapwings, there, and in a great many other
places as well, you will be sure to find skylarks, for they are almost
the commonest of our British birds. Certainly they are the ones that
we should miss the most if by some dreadful catastrophe they were
all to disappear. It does not seem to matter whether it is winter or
summer, spring or autumn: whether you are in the heart of the
country or on a common on the outskirts of some great city: whether
you are inland or by the sea.

Wherever you may find yourself, provided only there is a faint
gleam of sunshine, you may almost always hear a lark overhead, see
one mounting up and up, trilling away in the most joyous and
unceasing of all bird songs. Or if it is raining, you may still see the
lark, a cheerful figure with his or her jaunty little crest of feathers,
bustling along on the ground, finding a meal of small insects,
especially tiny beetles, if it be summer time, or in winter making

himself content with seeds of all kinds. Winter or summer, plenty of grit is eaten as well. Only when thick snow covers the ground is the lark at a loss, and at that time, though he is really a resident all the year round in this country, some of our larks migrate west to Ireland, returning in the early spring, whilst birds from further east come to England .

Perhaps he is not a showy bird to look at. Just as the nightingale has a song which is more beautiful than his appearance, so the lark does not go in for fine feathers. Yet he is so neat and dapper and cheerful that you cannot help looking again at his gay little brown crest, the light brown, streaked with darker, of his head and body, the pale stripe under his eye, and the buffish-white underpart, streaked and spotted with darker colour on the breast. In the autumn, after they have moulted, the brown feathers take on a redder tinge, partly, perhaps, looking brighter because the edges of the wings show almost white at that time. The nestlings are very much the same in colour, only the streaks and bars are less distinct; most attractive little things they are, whether you find four or five of them snuggled up in the nest on the ground, or chance to come on one of them fully fledged and wandering about a little forlornly outside.

Few of the birds who build on the ground make so pretty and perfect a nest as the skylark, many of them, like the lapwing, seeming content to lay the eggs in any shallow depression with practically nothing in the way of a nest. But then the lapwing is hatched with a good covering of down and can run quite strongly from the very first; skylarks, on the other hand, like young thrushes, blackbirds, and other birds who are hatched in comfortable nests, are helpless, blind, and with only the skimpiest covering of down. So it is really necessary for them to have a substantial nursery. A lark's nest certainly answers to that description, for it is made of dry grass lined with finer grasses, and is often placed under a protecting tussock of grass, or in a little hollow made by the bird in the furrows of a ploughed field...

Watch the care with which the parents leave the nest – for both take their turn at sitting and at singing. Off the eggs she slips, runs quickly a few yards through the grass or furrows, so that you may be deceived as to the exact whereabouts of the nest, and then, with a light little flutter, mounts into the air, beginning, quite possibly, to sing when only a few feet above the ground, and continuing, on and on, until you can see no bird in the height of sky above you, only you can hear that lovely, happy trilling coming back to you from the blue. Presently you may see the bird come down again, still singing. Perhaps she makes a rapid descent, almost like a fall, for a certain distance, and then soars again suddenly for a little way before she finally comes to earth, again a little distance from the nest, to which she will run off, full of importance, yet still full of wariness that you shall not make out where she goes.

Yet larks do not only sing to their mates on the nest, but at all other times as well, just as if they were so happy that all the world must share delight with them. The nightingale only sings his lovely song whilst his mate is sitting, and stops when the young hatch, beginning again if the nestlings should meet with disaster so that his mate starts again with a fresh nest. But the lark sings all the time, all the year round except just when moulting. Don't you think that splendid happiness is enough to make us put the lark first of British song birds, the one which we could least do without ?

Eleanor E. Helme

The skylark came

With its effort hooked to the sun, a swinging ladder

With its song
A labour of its whole body
Thatching the sun with bird-joy

To keep off the rains of weariness
The snows of extinction

With its labour
Of a useless excess, lifting what can only fall

With its crest
Which it intends to put on the sun

Which it meanwhile wears itself
so earth can be crested

With its song
Erected between dark and dark

The lark that lives and dies
In the service of its crest.

Ted Hughes
(1930–   )

Praying

As lark ascending
Ending in air
Sings its song there,
If sounds I am sending
Don't go anywhere
I seem not to care.

After singing the lark
Drops back to the ground.
I cover my dark
With the palm of a hand
As horses in fields suddenly stop
Their gallop at a horizon and crop.

P.J. Kavanagh
(1931–   )

The skylark and the steeplejack

I hope that I shall not be guilty of transgression by relating a simple and perfectly true story, with the object of showing the depth of feeling and tender sentiment a rough hewn man can reveal toward a small creature companion – a little bird.

Somewhere in Leicestershire two Steeplejacks were at work near the top of a Church spire.

'Blime, Bill! 'ow do yer reckon this 'ere got 'ere?' asked one, of his mate, as he held up a small tin box which he had discovered behind some loose mortar. Opening the box the men were amazed to see the remains of a small bird, packed, with apparent care, in some soft material.

Now this is really an imaginary ending to the story – a probable happening at some time in the future. The following is a true revelation of a mystery to come.

I had the story direct from the hero thereof – a young Steeplejack known for his nerve and daring, during a rare outpouring of confidences. I believe that I alone now hold the secret as the poor fellow later met with a fatal accident during his hazardous employment.

He owned a Skylark he had reared from young and to which he was much attached. One sad day a cat so injured the bird that it died.

The Steeplejack spent days of dejection, he confessed, carrying the bird in his pocket the while. What follows had best be told in his words, as far as I can recollect them:-

'At dinner time, when my mates went to get some beer down 'em, I went up the spire we was repairing. I went secret like and feeling like a silly kid. 'Cheerio! pal,' I said when I tucked 'im away up there. 'You don't want to rot in no earth.' Funny! but somehow that bit of silly fooling seemed to buck me up no end.'

James Herne

The skylark

Many years ago I flushed a Skylark from its nest of four eggs when hunting for those of a Ringed Plover on Luffness Links near the now very fashionable East Scottish golfing resorts of Gullane and North Berwick. I had my camera with me, and I shall always remember the difficulty I had to obtain what I took to be a correct 'nest and eggs' photograph. Since that time I have found many nests of this charming and well-known songster, in the Shetlands, in Southern Scotland, Norfolk, the home counties and elsewhere: in all these areas I am glad to say I found it common.

I do not know of any other species whose young ones are better arrayed to conceal them from their enemies. The nest which illustrates this chapter (Plates 28–30) was a very striking example of this 'protective coloration,' an expression I do not care for, but I think it describes the position, if not better, anyway as well as any other. I had watched this pair of Skylarks for some time, and I had seen them carrying food. Both birds returned frequently to the same area, but not at an exact spot. This rather intrigued me, and made me wonder if their young ones had already left the nest. After a time I decided to discover for myself whether my surmise was correct or not.

After much searching I nearly trod on the nest with its complement of baby Larks. I know many of the really experienced bird men will scoff at this, but as I said in my preface, I am only stating my own experiences, stupid as they may seem to some, but definitely interesting to me myself and, I hope, to others as well. When the photographs are examined, I think many will agree that these young Larks, packed tightly in their nest, dead still except for their quick breathing, and with their marvellous resemblance to the grasses around them, even to the little stiff pieces sticking out, which in the chicks is a speckly down, were a thing which could easily be passed. This is as Nature meant it to be. The old birds had not landed directly at the nest, but some distance away, and then had run to their young ones and fed them. It was really when they left that they gave their secret away, as they nearly always took wing as soon as they had disposed of the latest meal, without taking the precaution of running some distance as on their arrival. How often I have seen this failing, for this is how I look upon it. Even a bird like the Grasshopper Warbler, which appears to have long tunnels or passages to its nest, leaves close by them when feeding young ones.

As soon as I could do it, I put my hide up at this nest, and when searching for material with which to cover it up, saw the old birds go down to the nest without any hesitation. I, therefore, did not see any reason for covering things up, and got into the hide at once. I had not been left more than ten minutes, when I heard the very cheery *'cheer-up'* of one of the birds, and with that the nest and its contents were transformed from part of the surrounding country to an excited mass of mouths and flutterings, which became more animated the closer their parent came, chirruping all the way. Out of my peephole I saw her threading her way through the grasses, and it was only for a moment that she hesitated before feeding the family. Immediately away she flew, and the nest and its contents once more merged into the grassy surroundings. Not for long, however, because the cock arrived, his beak crammed with flies. In spite of this he was able to announce his close arrival by actually singing a very low stanza of his well-known song. With his crest fully raised, he arrived from a different direction to his mate, and, standing at the back and above the nest, awkwardly fed his chicks from this lofty position. So very like a male to do such a thing awkwardly, when his hen approached on the level and made things much less strenuous for both herself and the youngsters.

When the young ones of the ground breeding birds like the Lark or Yellow Wagtail are nearly due to leave their nest, their excitement is so great when the old birds arrive with food, that they run out to meet them. One Lark's nest that I watched had young birds on the point of departure, and as soon as they even heard a parent in the offing, they would dash from the tuft in which the nest was placed on to a piece of ground a few feet away with very short grass. The thing that impressed me most was the apparent inability of these young Larks to determine whence their parents were coming. They would run out in all directions, and appeared to me to show surprise if they had taken the wrong line and missed a meal. Owing to these youngsters being almost full grown I could not photograph them, as they would have flown from the nest if I had attempted to remove even one or two grasses, and this would have been necessary to show them properly. I watched them from a very low hide some distance away. The birds I photographed had flown when I returned a few days later, and I was not able to obtain them running out to meet their parents as I had hoped.

Every year a pair of Larks nest on a small piece of waste land which I pass twice daily on my way to and from the station. Gradually houses are springing up on this, and I wonder how much longer I shall be able to enjoy the glorious song of the male bird, as he rises on joyous wings higher and higher into the heavens, pouring out his very soul, it seems, in ecstasy to his sitting mate. How often I have nearly missed that train by watching his ascent and descent with its final plunge to earth, singing all the time.

Ian M. Thomson

The skylark

I used to go to the meadows in May to listen to the skylarks. There are usually three pairs in the first meadow and at least four in the next, so on warm sunny days when all the cocks are singing the air is full of delightful sounds.

They never begin at the same moment, of course, though sometimes there is a difference of only a few notes between them. Usually one will spring into the air and when he has got well started, a second will follow. Then at intervals the rest, one after another will take up the challenge. And as each of them sings for ten or twenty minutes without a pause and begins again after a short rest, the music goes on for hours.

On such days I sometimes lay on my back and watched them as they soared higher and higher until they seemed to disappear in the blue of the sky, and then picked them out again as they began to descend and followed them until they disappeared among the long grass. I thought of the blackbird, thrush, starling and others which sing while they are resting, I remembered that the tits sing while at work and that this makes a difference in the quality of their notes. I recalled, too, the gay, clever and boastful chaffinch and the proud and assertive wren.

Of them all the thrush comes nearest to the skylark. He makes a joyful noise and he shows this in the tilt of his head as he shouts out his ringing notes. But the skylark's song is a flood of gladness. He cannot remember the rigours of last winter, but he feels his present freedom. It is good to be alive and well in a land of plenty and to feel and enjoy the warmth and brightness of the sunshine, so he lifts up his heart and rejoices.

And he lifts it up to some purpose. For here is a little perching bird who has given up perching. He prefers to roost on the ground under the shelter of a tuft of grass or in the hollow of a turf. The branches of trees may be safe from prowling and swooping enemies, but there are other things in life that are more worth than safety.

Besides, when a great little heart is bubbling over with gladness, branches are a hindrance. For him the top most twig of the tallest tree is no better than a blade of grass; indeed, to sit on it would be to suffer the pangs of imprisonment. The sky is his kingdom and he must soar to possess it.

But there is more in it than that. Other birds soar and show in their actions that they are enjoying the experience. It is not for the pleasure of soaring that the skylark seeks the sky; he soars to express himself. As he mounts up, his every movement is full of passion. His head swings from side to side as he throws out his flood of song, and there is a peculiar quality in the beating of his wings which is not present in his ordinary flight. An old poet who was a good observer of Nature, says that he 'shakes his wings.' In fact he is not so much soaring and singing as singing and dancing. It is not enough that he should sing his heart out, he must dance it out as well. Hence the need for the wide, unbroken spaces in which he has chosen to live, and the open sky...

Most singing birds are sun lovers. They show this when the days are longest, for it is then that they sing a wonderful chorus at dawn. Like some human choruses this is introduced by several soloists, and it does not reach its full volume until the sun has begun to rise. Some of these soloists start when the first grey tint appears in the east, but there is one that may be heard earlier than that. In the darkness that precedes the dawn I have heard the skylark singing and I have not counted him as a songster of the night. As he mounted higher and higher, I have thought of that bold spirit looking over the rim of the world and greeting the approaching sun.

I have listened to his song, too, after the last ray of daylight had vanished and I have not then classed him with the nightingale, which hides himself in a thicket and shouts as timid people do in the dark. The skylark had sung and danced joyously all day in the glorious summer sunshine, and now he was bravely overtopping the night to prolong his jubilation and in the end to bid *au revoir* to the wonderful source of his happiness.

C. S. Bayne

Sky-lark

The sky-Lark seems to belong more to heaven than to earth. When he sings near to earth without soaring, the song lacks its fervour. Always a wing tremolo – or vibrato – accompanies his flight-song. I have seen a Lark singing his full song facing a strong breeze drifting slowly backwards on tremulous wings. When the field hedge was below him the song and wing fluttering suddenly ceased, and he flew quickly forward against the wind, with fast but firmly-beating wings alternating between rests with wings closed, a dipping flight accompanied by his call-note, 'seep, seep'. They have a short little song, sung close to the ground or when chasing each other, this seeming conversational and an extension of one of their call-notes – the trill call-note.

Lark music has special significance for me. One of the great experiences of my life was when I first heard the song, at the age of about eleven, with full realisation of its beauty. I was lying on the slopes of a sand-dune, a book opened to start reading, when the Lark's song suddenly held me; while the bird soared far into the sky overhead his music brought a glorious revelation of beauty, not only for its own sake, but because it seemed the true meaning of life. Certain details of the scene remain vividly clear, especially the marramgrass tufts on the high sand-hill above me, the last pinnacle of earth beyond which was the blue sky, the lark's world.

A bird, in spite of the inspirational power of his song, is generally supposed to be devoid of the immortal soul accredited to man. Among those who feel strongly the spiritual appeal of bird-song there must be some who ponder this question: How can bird-music have this great power to move a human soul unless a bird's spirit released in song, is component with the Divine?

> *The starry voice ascending spreads,*
> *Awakening, as it waxes thin,*
> *The best in us to him akin:*

Our wisdom speaks from failing blood,
Our passion is too full in flood,
We want the key of his wild note
Of truthful in a tuneful throat.

Larks

The larks are small drab birds but what they lack in plumage, they make up for with their superb song. They will pour forth their song whether on vibrating wings or from a post or a bush.

The family is almost exclusively confined to the Old World and is best established in Africa although two species have established themselves in Australia and one (the horned lark) has succeeded in reaching the New World. This attractive species, with its black 'whiskers' and 'horns' is found throughout North America to southern Mexico and one isolated population is to be found in the Colombian highlands in South America. In Europe it is known as the shore lark.

Larks are birds of open terrain, although thin bush-like territory is tolerated living on plains, moorlands, cultivated fields, deserts or beaches. They are not found in forests, woods or jungle country. They are well adapted for a life on open land, using the sky or a simple bush or post to indicate their territory. They make good use of the protective hues of the plumage; indeed for a group of birds which live in open country, this must be all important.

When alarmed a lark will run or fly a short distance, then crouch low before running again. The running speed of some larks is at least five m.p.h....

Matthew J. Brennan

The Skylark

The Skylark, fairly small and with unobtrusive colouring, is virtually invisible as you casually scan the ploughland or pasture where it is feeding, alone, with its mate or, in winter, in a small flock. But few people have not seen and heard what happens next – and it can happen on almost any day in the year.

Near a downland village in Berkshire which I often visit, a lane winds steeply uphill from a secluded dry valley. There are hawthorn thickets by the road and farm fields on either side. Often, just as I have reached the highest point on the great sweeping hillside to turn the corner and go downhill again to the village, a Skylark rises vertically from the field on my left, with a continuous stream of trilled, gliding or staccato sound as it goes up and up. Then it hovers, singing and beating its wings, sometimes circling over the field. Before it has risen far its rival on the other side of the road is airborne too. They sing against each other for minutes on end, until the pattern of notes and phrases changes as they come down, giving a few final song notes before the last, sudden, and silent, drop to the ground.

In the same fields there are often Lapwings, or Green Plovers, as they are called: larger, more powerful birds than the Skylark and with an impressive presence – black throat and head, surmounted by a delicate crest; white on their cheeks and underparts; their back and wings glinting green and purple, and a chestnut-coloured patch under the tail. Their outline and colour show up in striking contrast with the ground as they parade about the fields, slowly and with dignity, stopping from time to time to feed or preen.

For most of the year Lapwings live in large flocks. They will not allow an intruder to approach too closely and take to the air immediately. relying on numbers and aerial agility, not on concealment for safety. In autumn they execute great flock manoeuvres in the air, the black and white plumage patterns changing as they wheel and alter direction of flight. Like the Skylarks, they may move over considerable distances, feeding on moorlands and tidal flats as well as cultivated fields...

The various displays of the Lapwing and the Skylark resemble each other in little but their use of aerial space above an open ground habitat. Different habits, and spectacular plumage in one species, unspectacular in the other, are associated with a different balance between vocal and visual signals...

The analysis of the songs of many species in terms of sound alone is a necessary first step towards a better understanding of the formal resemblances between bird music and human music. Professor Hartshorne, in his book *Born to Sing* has made a magnificent beginning with a worldwide survey of all the birdsongs known from the ever-lengthening catalogue of recordings, or from adequate field descriptions.

By applying standard criteria to the evaluation of songs and assessing characteristics such as complexity, organization and tone-quality, some of which are measurable, he has tried to rid the process of comparison of vague, subjective judgements such as 'beautiful' or 'musical'. He has made a list, compiled on this basis, of the 200 or so best singers of the world among approximately 5000 species which can be said to sing.

This list, incidentally, includes nine species that breed in the British Isles: the Nightingale, Robin, Blackbird and Song Thrush; the Garden Warbler, Marsh Warbler and Blackcap; the Skylark and Woodlark. Our runners-up – good but not superlative singers – are the Sedge Warbler, Tree Pipit, Pied Flycatcher and, more doubtfully, the Dipper and the Linnet. This selection accords well with the song-ratings of earlier authorities who had perforce to confine themselves to a smaller number of species, and often to regional groups, within their travelling experience. Most bird-listeners in Britain would agree with the choice.

Rosemary Jellis

Larks and the ladys' hawk...

The merlin, our smallest native falcon used in hawking, was reserved in medieval times for noble and sporting ladies – appropriate for a charming and dainty little falcon.

Its specialty was the skylark, and this often meant a high ringing flight into the blue sky over open moors or grassland. Salisbury Plain was a favourite area for this particular form of falconry, particularly among members of the Old Hawking Club earlier this century.

Lark-hawking with merlins is still carried on by a few dedicated enthusiasts, but skylarks and merlins are both now governed by strict licensing regulations by the Dept of the Environment.

from *The Field*

The skylark

Soaring higher and higher until it becomes a barely visible speck, hundreds of feet above the ground, the skylark sings its long and unforgettable warbling song. This joyful melody, much celebrated in literature and music, is performed during the bird's stunning aerobatic display and serves to stake out a territorial claim, as well as to advertise the presence of a mature breeding male to females of similar intent.

Most bird sing from fixed song posts such as fences or trees, but the skylark, essentially a ground-living, low-flying bird, has little use for such pedestrian props. With the sky as its stage the lark hovers above its territory, and performs its liquid love song for up to five minutes.

The skylark's spectacular upward fight in full song with wings a-blur as it powers itself ever higher, is equally matched by the drama of its descent. Still singing, it suddenly plummets downwards with wings folded, seemingly locked into a death-defying dive. Before it reaches the earth, however, it calmly straightens out and with wings flapping and tail spread it drops gently to the ground as if supported by an invisible parachute.

Rising on a tide of sound, the skylark is one of the 'early birds', starting its day singing while most other birds are still dozing in the twilight and giving credence to the country expression 'up with the lark'. Fortunately for such an early riser its song is both varied and musical.

During the breeding season the female sky-lark makes a nest on the ground. The cup-shaped nest is woven from grass and often lined with hair. Sometimes the nest is sheltered by a tuft of grass but usually it is out in the open. From late April onwards in fairly rapid succession the hen lays two or three clutches of at least 3–4 eggs which she incubates for about 11 days. The newly-hatched chicks are fed in the nest by both parent birds for about 10 days. Soon after, the young birds leave the nest, flying for the first time 16 days later.

By the end of the autumn the resident skylark population of two to four million pairs is temporarily swelled, not only by the summer's fledglings but also by a tremendous influx of migrant skylarks from the Continent which winter in Britain.

ALARMING LOSS OF HABITAT

At one time, the chalky uplands which are the skylark's ideal habitat were vast tracts of undulating grassland used as pasturage for roving flocks of sheep. Today much downland is now under the plough and producing wheat and barley. Although skylarks are still to be found in these rolling hills they have been affected by this alarming loss of habitat and the number of breeding pairs has been significantly reduced. Worse still, in some areas this celebrated songster is even regarded as a serious agricultural pest. Before the introduction of uniformly spaced pelleted seed, farmers were prepared to tolerate the loss, to skylarks and other birds, of a small percentage of seedlings, which probably would have had to be thinned. Now, any seed loss is significant and large flocks of larks are no longer welcomed.

Yet while the farmers may try to discourage the skylark from settling in their fields, to kill them would be illegal. But during the 19th Century, lark catching was an important downland activity, with the coastal resort of Brighton the centre of activity. Massive slaughter still continues in Europe, and while it has long been banned in Britain, the steady destruction of the skylark's habitat may prove to be just as damaging to this high-flying minstrel of the downs.

BIBLIOGRAPHY

Studies of Sensation and Event (1843)
The Angler: Poetical Works of David Macbeth Moir (1852)
British Birds in their Haunts Rev'd C.A. Johns
(Routledge and Kegan Paul, 1861)
Wild Life in a Southern County Richard Jefferies (1879)
Tales of the Birds W. Warde Fowler (Macmillan & Co., 1889)
Lloyd's Encyclopedic Dictionary Edward Lloyd, (1985)
The Farmer and the Birds Edith Carrington
(George Bell & Sons Ltd., 1898)
The Poetical Works of Thomas Gray ed. John Bradshaw
(Macmillan & Co., London, 1891)
An American Anthology 1787–1900 ed. Stedman
(Houghton, Mifflin & Co., Riverside Press, Cambridge, USA, 1901)
The Roadmender Michael Fairless (Duckworth, 1902)
British Bird Life W. Percival Westell (T. Fisher Unwin, 1904)
Lucy Bettesworth George Bourne (Duckworth, 1913)
New Golden Treasury of Songs and Lyrics ed. Ernest Rhys
(Dent/Dutton, 1914)
Songs of the Birds Walter Garstang
(John Lane, The Bodley Head, 1922)
Georgian Poetry 1920–1922 (The Poetry Bookshop, 1922)
Poems about Birds ed. H.J. Massingham (T. Fisher Unwin, 1922)
A Treasury of Verse ed. M.G. Edgar/Eric Chilman
(George G. Harrap, 1925)
Feathered Friends of Field and Forest Eleanor E. Helme
(Religious Tract Society, 1926)
The Charm of Birds Edward Grey, 1st Viscount Fallodon
(Hodder & Stoughton, 1927)
Collected Poems Muriel Elsie Graham (Williams & Norgate, 1930)
The Village Book Henry Williamson (Jonathan Cape, 1930)
Birds from the Hide Ian M. Thomson (A. & C. Black, 1933)

Out of Doors with Richard Jefferies (J.M. Dent, 1935)
The Book of Nature W. Percival Westell
(Oxford University Press, 1935)
Nature All Around W.B. Little
(Sir Isaac Pitman & Sons Ltd., 1935)
The Desk Drawer Anthology ed. Alice Roosevelt Longworth/
Theodore Roosevelt. From poems submitted through
Alexander Woollcott (Hutchinson & Co., 1937)
Enid Blyton's Nature Lover's Book (Evans Brothers, 1944)
Getting to know the Birds C.S. Bayne (Collins, 1944)
Talking Out of Doors H.L. Gee (George Ronald, 1948)
These Also: An Anthology sel./arr. M.M. Johnson
(Cambridge University Press, 1945)
The Roadmender and Other Writings Michael Fairless
(Collins, 1950)
Birds as Individuals Len Howard (Collins, 1952)
Country Life ed. A.F. Scott (Macmillan & Co., 1952)
News from the Village Gerald Bullett
(Cambridge University Press, 1952)
The Greek Bucolic Poets transl. A.S.F. Gow
(Cambridge University Press, 1953)
A Treasury of Jewish Poetry Nathan & Marynn Ausubel
(Crown, NY, 1957)
The Bird-lover's Bedside Book ed. R.M. Lockley
(Eyre & Spottiswoode, 1958)
Birds, Beasts & Fishes compiled Ruth Manning-Sanders
(Oxford University Press, 1962)
The Animal Anthology ed. and prefaced Diana Spearman
(John Baker, 1966)
Bird Sounds and their Meaning Rosemary Jellis
(BBC Publications, 1977)
Poetry of the First World War (Wayland Publishers, 1988)

224

INDEX OF AUTHORS